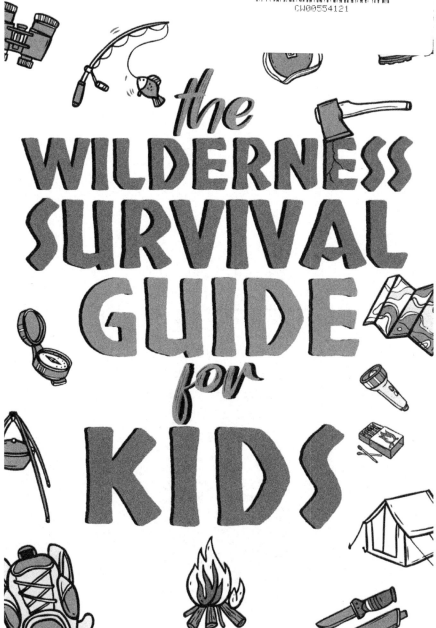

the WILDERNESS SURVIVAL GUIDE for KIDS

Please think about leaving a review at:

US - mightymammothpress.org/review
UK - mightymammothpress.org/review-uk

For any questions, please contact us at:
support@mightymammothpress.org

ISBN: 978-1-913485-41-2
© 2024, Mighty Mammoth Press.
All rights reserved.

SCAN TO GET
OUR NEXT BOOK
ABSOLUTELY
FREE

Contents

Introduction..1

Chapter 1: Basic Wilderness Safety 5

    Tell Someone Where You're Going 7
    Safety In Numbers (Adventure Together) 9
    How To Plan (Fail To Plan, Plan To Fail) 11
    Pack Right, But Stay Light 13
    Dress For Survival.. 16
    Be Respectful Of Nature.. 19
    Take Enough Water.. 21

Chapter 2: How To Find Water...23

    Hydration Is Key: Why Water Is Critical For Wilderness Survival...............25
    How To Find Water Sources In The Wild......................................27
    Methods Of Water Purification 29
    Other Tips And Tricks To Finding Water 31

Chapter 3: Securing Or Building A Shelter 33

    Types Of Shelters 35
    How To Build A Survival Shelter 37
    Which Tent Should I Buy? 39
    Location, Location, Location 41

Chapter 4: How To Make A Fire..43

    Techniques For Starting A Fire... 45
    Natural Fire Starters.. 47
    Fire-Building Structures 50
    Weather Considerations 53
    Extinguishing And Leaving No Trace 56
    Stay Safe And Protect The Environment..................................... 58

Chapter 5: Looking For Food 61

Foraging With Care 63

Seasonal Foraging: Nature's Calendar 65

Safe Foraging Practices 68

Edible Insects: A Tiny Feast 71

Cooking In The Wild 75

Hunting Animals For Survival...78

Chapter 6: Finding Your Way 81

What To Do If You Are Lost? 83

Using The Sky 86

Landmarks And Terrain Features 89

Staying On Track 91

Modern Technology In Navigation 93

Chapter 7: Wilderness First Aid 95

Cuts And Scrapes: Treating Minor Wounds And Preventing Infection.........99

Treating Common Injuries: Practical Treatment Techniques 101

Infection Watch: Identifying And Responding To Signs Of Infection 103

Why A First Aid Kit Is A Must! 106

Chapter 8: Wilderness Communication 109

Basic Wilderness Communication Tools 111

How To Signal Sos In Different Forms... 113

Basic Morse Code.. 116

Using Technology Wisely 119

Emergency Phone Numbers.. 121

Chapter 9: Mental Toughness... 123

Stress Management In The Wild 125

Goal Setting And Personal Challenges... 127

Handling Isolation 129

Conclusion 131

INTRODUCTION

Adventure Awaits

Picture this: You're about to step into the great outdoors, armed not just with a backpack but with super cool skills that make you feel like a wilderness detective. This isn't just about surviving on a deserted island; it's about turning every little outdoor hiccup into an epic win. Even though heaps of us love the thought of exploring the wild, many young adventurers (yep, that's you!) aged 8 to 16 find themselves a tad unsure about what to do when Mother Nature throws a curveball.

Fear to Fun

This book is like your secret map to treasure, teaching you awesome survival skills that are super handy not just in the deep, dark woods but also in your backyard adventures. We're talking about turning "Uh-oh" moments into "Aha!" moments, swapping fear for fun, and transforming curiosity into your superpower.

Brave Explorers Wanted

The great outdoors is vast and full of mysteries, which can be both wildly exciting and a wee bit scary. Thoughts like "What if I get lost?" or "What's that rustling in the bushes?" might pop up. But guess what? That mix of thrill and worry is the first step to becoming an adventure champ. This book gears you up with the know-how to dance in the rain (literally), chat with the stars, and even decode the secret language of the forest.

Time to Skill-up

- **Water Whiz**: Dive into the science of staying hydrated with experiments that are more fun than a water balloon fight.

- **Fire Master:** Learn the secrets of sparking a fire that would make even dragons jealous, all while being the safest firebug around.

- **Pathfinder Pro**: With or without a compass, discover how to use the sun, stars, and even trees to guide your way like an ancient explorer.

- **Shelter Superstar**. Learn to craft survival shelters using nature's bounty for the ultimate wilderness hideaway.

- **Signal Savvy**. Master wilderness communication with tools and techniques—from SOS signals and Morse code to smart tech use and emergency contacts, ensuring you're always heard.

Each chapter is like a game level, helping you master these skills in a way that sticks, packed with fun facts, DIYs, and brain teasers that make learning a blast.

Level Up in Life

As you master these outdoor skills, you're also unlocking secret levels in the game of life. Building a fire or reading a compass doesn't just mean you're ready for adventure; it means you're growing into a super confident, problem-solving, can-do wizard.

Team Up for Adventure

This book isn't just for solo adventurers; it's a ticket to epic family quests. In a world where screens often steal the show, these survival skills invite you and your crew (a.k.a. your family) to log off and dive into real-life adventures. Imagine the stories you'll tell after a day of constellation spotting, backyard camping, or even a treasure hunt using your new navigation skills. It's all about laughs, teamwork, and high-fives all around.

Nature's Reset Button

Stepping into nature with your new skills is like hitting the reset button. Feeling the wind, listening to a stream, or just getting your hands dirty can wash away stress and bring a big ol' smile to your face. It's about being in the moment, forgetting about homework (just for a bit!), and feeling all kinds of good vibes.

Join the Adventure Club

So, are you ready to jump into a world where learning feels like playing the coolest game ever? This book is your golden ticket to becoming a confident, joy-spreading, adventure-loving explorer of the great outdoors – and of life itself.

Grab your explorer's hat (or make one!), open this book, and let's kick off an adventure that's all about fun, skills, and making memories. The path to becoming a fearless explorer, an awesome family teammate, and a happy nature nerd starts right here. Let's dive into this adventure today – because everyone from 8 to 16 deserves to be a hero in the great big world of the outdoors!

CHAPTER 1

BASIC WILDERNESS SAFETY

When we step into the great outdoors, it's a whole new world out there! It's exciting, but we need to be smart and safe. So, let's dive right in and learn how to enjoy nature safely.

First things first, always tell someone where you're going. It's like leaving a little map of your adventure with a friend or family. This way, if you're out longer than expected, someone knows where to find you.

It's also super cool to have a buddy with you. Why? Because two heads are better than one, especially when exploring new places. Plus, it's way more fun!

Now, let's talk about planning. Before you even pack your backpack, figure out where you're going and check the weather. It's like being a detective and a weather reporter all in one. No surprises means a better adventure.

Speaking of packing, remember the rule: pack right, but stay light. You'll need some essentials like a first aid kit, matches, and a map, but leave behind stuff you won't use. It's like going on a treasure hunt, only taking what you really need.

Dress smart too. It might not be the latest fashion, but wearing the right clothes can make a big difference. Think comfy and safe, not just cool.

Being respectful of nature is key. Imagine nature as a giant, beautiful museum. You can look, take photos, but don't take anything else. This way, it stays awesome for everyone.

Lastly, don't forget water. It's the most important thing you'll carry. You can never have too much of it. It's like carrying a little life-saver in your bottle.

There you have it! Basic wilderness safety isn't hard, it's just about being smart, prepared, and respectful. Let's keep safe and have the best time out there!

TELL SOMEONE WHERE YOU'RE GOING

Heading out for an adventure in the great outdoors can be thrilling. Whether it's a trek through the woods or a day at the park, one simple step can make all the difference: telling someone where you're going. This isn't just a rule; it's a smart move, a safety net that every wise adventurer keeps ready.

Why is this so important? Think of it as leaving a breadcrumb trail, not of actual breadcrumbs (because that would be weird and not good for nature), but a trail of information. This trail tells someone you trust — maybe a parent, a friend, or a neighbor — exactly where you plan to be. Whether it's hiking up the sunny trails of Pine Ridge or exploring the grassy fields of Green Meadow Park, they know.

The beauty of this simple act is in its power. If, for some reason, the adventure takes a bit longer, or if something unexpected happens, someone knows where to start looking. It's not about expecting trouble; it's about being prepared, like a superhero who plans ahead.

Now, how do you do this? It's easy. Before you zip up your backpack and step out, take a moment. Tell someone the plan. Where are you going? Which paths will you take? When do you expect to be back? This chat doesn't need to be long, just clear and complete. It's like giving them a map of your day.

Remember, adventures are about freedom, fun, and exploring, but they're also about being smart. The world outside is vast, filled with wonders and surprises. By letting someone know your plans, you're not just taking care of yourself; you're giving peace of mind to those who care about you.

This practice also teaches responsibility. It shows you're thinking ahead, considering others, and taking charge of your safety. These are big, important skills — the kind that don't just apply to adventures in nature but to everyday life as well.

And there's a bonus. Once you've told someone where you're going, you can dive into your adventure with a light heart. You're free to focus on the chirping birds, the rustling leaves, and the cool breeze. You can chase butterflies, watch squirrels, or gaze at the clouds without a worry. Your mind is clear to soak in every moment, every new discovery.

So, next time you're ready to step out and embrace the world's natural playground, pause for a moment. Share your plans. It's a small step, but it's a giant leap in being a smart, responsible adventurer. It's a habit that marks the beginning of countless safe and joyous explorations.

In the world of outdoor adventures, this is the golden rule. It's a rule that ensures adventures remain what they're meant to be — fun, exciting, and safe. So, tell someone where you're going, and then, with a heart full of excitement, step into your adventure, ready to explore, learn, and grow.

SAFETY IN NUMBERS
(ADVENTURE TOGETHER)

There's a saying that goes, 'Two heads are better than one.' When it comes to exploring the outdoors, this couldn't be truer. Adventure is always more fun and safer with friends or family. The idea of 'safety in numbers' is not just a saying; it's a smart way to enjoy adventures.

Think about a flock of birds flying together or a pack of wolves. They stick together for a reason. When you're with others, you have more eyes to spot exciting things and more brains to solve problems. If you're trying to figure out which way the trail goes or if you need to build a shelter, it's always easier and more fun when you're not alone.

Being with a group also means you can help each other. If one of you gets tired, the others can offer a hand. If someone forgets their water bottle, you can share. It's about looking out for each other, like a team of explorers on a grand expedition.

When you're planning a trip into nature, think about who you can bring along. Maybe it's your best friend who loves to spot different kinds of birds. Or your cousin who knows a lot about trees. Or even your little sister who's great at finding cool rocks. Each person can bring something unique to the adventure.

And there's something special about sharing experiences. When you see a beautiful waterfall or a deer in the woods, it's so much better when you can turn to someone and say, 'Did you see that?' Those shared moments become memories that last a lifetime.

Having more people also means you can try bigger and more exciting things. Maybe you can't cross a stream on your own, but with friends, you can find a way together. Or maybe you're a bit scared to try climbing a hill, but with your family cheering you on, you feel brave enough to try.

It's also about learning from each other. Maybe your friend knows how to read a compass, and they can teach you. Or you know how to spot animal tracks, and you can show them. It's like each adventure is a chance to learn something new, not just about nature, but from each other.

But remember, more people also mean more responsibility. You have to make sure everyone stays together and nobody gets left behind. It's like being the captain of a ship or the leader of an expedition. You have to make sure everyone is safe and happy.

When you go on adventures with others, it's not just about where you go or what you see. It's about the laughs you share, the challenges you overcome together, and the stories you'll tell later. It's about building friendships and learning to work as a team.

So next time you're thinking of heading out into the wild, don't go it alone. Bring your friends, your family, or anyone who loves adventure as much as you do. Together, you'll not only be safer, but you'll also have more fun. Because in the end, the best adventures are the ones we share.

HOW TO PLAN (FAIL TO PLAN, PLAN TO FAIL)

Setting off on an outdoor adventure? Great! But wait, have you planned your trip? Planning might sound boring, but it's the secret sauce to a fantastic and safe adventure. It's like being a detective and a captain all in one. Let's break it down into easy steps to make sure your trip is a hit!

Step 1: Choosing Your Destination: First, decide where you're going. Are you hiking in the hills, camping in the forest, or exploring a local park? Get a map of the place and study it. Look for trails, landmarks, and interesting spots. Knowing your destination well means fewer surprises.

Step 2: Plan Your Route: Next up, plan your route. It's like drawing a treasure map. Where will you start? Where will you stop for lunch? Which paths will you take? Marking your route helps you stay on track. It also lets you estimate how long your adventure will take.

Step 3: Check the Weather: Weather can change your plans in a flash. A sunny morning can turn into a rainy afternoon. So, check the weather forecast. It helps you decide what to wear and what to pack. If the weather looks bad, it's smarter to change your plans. After all, the hills aren't going anywhere!

Step 4: What to Pack: Packing is an art. You need enough to be prepared, but not so much that your backpack feels like a bag of bricks. Essentials include water, snacks, a first aid kit, a map, and a compass. Dress in layers and bring a raincoat — just in case. And don't forget a hat and sunscreen.

Step 5: Telling Someone Your Plan: Always tell someone about your plan. Let them know where you're going and when you'll be back. It's a safety step you shouldn't skip.

Step 6: Preparing for Emergencies: Even with the best plans, things can go sideways. What if you get lost or hurt? Have a plan. Carry a whistle — three blasts are a universal call for help. Know basic first aid. And if you're lost, stay put. It's easier to find someone who isn't moving.

Step 7: Food and Water: Pack enough food for your trip and a little extra. Choose foods that are light but energy-boosting. Water is crucial. Bring plenty and then some. Staying hydrated keeps you sharp and energetic.

Step 8: Check Your Gear: Before you leave, check your gear. Is your backpack comfortable? Do your shoes fit well? Is your water bottle full? A quick check can save a lot of trouble later.

Step 9: Know the Local Wildlife: Read up on the wildlife in the area. It's important to know what animals you might encounter and how to be safe around them. Remember, you're a visitor in their home.

Step 10: Respect the Environment: While you're out there, respect nature. Stay on trails, don't disturb animals, and take your trash back with you. It's about leaving the place as beautiful as you found it.

Step 11: Enjoy and Learn: Finally, while you're busy exploring and having fun, don't forget to learn. Look around, ask questions, and soak in the beauty of nature. Every trip is a chance to learn something new.

Planning might take a bit of time, but it makes your adventure safer, smoother, and more fun. It turns you from a tourist into an explorer. So, take the time to plan. Your adventure will be all the better for it!

PACK RIGHT, BUT STAY LIGHT (PACKING ADVICE, CHECKLIST)

Packing for an outdoor adventure is like putting together a puzzle. Each piece is important, and you have to fit everything just right. The trick is to pack everything you need, but not so much that your backpack feels like you're carrying a mountain.

The Essentials: What You Must Bring

- **Water and Snacks:** You can't have an adventure without energy. Water keeps you hydrated, and snacks keep your energy up. Pack enough water for the trip and some extra, just in case. For snacks, think light but filling — like granola bars or fruit.

- **First Aid Kit:** Safety first! A basic first aid kit should have band-aids, antiseptic wipes, and some bandages. It's small but can be a real lifesaver.

- **Map and Compass:** Even if you know the area, a map and compass are must-haves. They're your guides when signs are scarce and cell phones don't work.

- **Matches or a Lighter:** If you need to make a fire, you'll need a way to start it. Waterproof matches or a reliable lighter are your best bets.

- **A Whistle:** Three blasts on a whistle is a universal call for help. It's loud, clear, and can be heard from far away.

Clothes

- **Layers are Key:** The weather can change quickly outdoors. Dress in layers so you can adjust to the temperature. Start with a base layer that keeps you dry, add an insulating layer for warmth, and top it off with a waterproof layer.

- **Hat and Gloves:** These aren't just for winter. A hat can protect you from the sun, and gloves can save your hands from scratches and cold.

Tools and Extras

- **A Knife or Multi-tool:** A small knife or a multi-tool can be handy for cutting, fixing, and a lot of unexpected tasks.

- **Flashlight or Headlamp:** If you're out past sunset, you'll need light. A small flashlight or a headlamp is a great idea. Don't forget extra batteries.

What Not to Pack

- **Too Many Clothes:** You don't need a whole wardrobe. Pick versatile pieces that can handle a bit of dirt.

- **Heavy Books or Gadgets:** Leave the heavy stuff at home. The best part of an adventure is disconnecting from screens and enjoying nature.

- **Fragile Items:** Anything that can break easily has no place in your backpack. Keep it simple and sturdy.

Packing Your Backpack

- **Balance is Key:** Put the heaviest items in the middle of your backpack, close to your back. Distribute the weight evenly so it's easier to carry.

- **Use all Space:** Roll your clothes to save space. Use pockets for small items. Think like you're playing a game of Tetris.

Double-Check Before You Leave! Before you head out, give your pack a quick check. Do you have everything? Is anything leaking or too heavy? A quick check can prevent problems later.

Packing might seem like a chore, but it's a crucial part of your adventure. It's about being prepared, safe, and comfortable. When you pack right and stay light, you set yourself up for an unforgettable experience in the great outdoors. So, pack smart, and then step into your adventure with confidence!

DRESS FOR SURVIVAL
(FUNCTION OVER FASHION)

When you're getting ready for an outdoor adventure, the clothes you choose are more than just outfits. They're your armor against the elements, your comfort during long hikes, and sometimes, they're even your lifesaver. Dressing for survival is about choosing function over fashion, making sure you're prepared for whatever Mother Nature throws your way.

Layer Up! - The secret to dressing for the outdoors is layers. Layers keep you warm, but they can also be removed if you get too hot. Start with a base layer. This isn't just any shirt; it's one that wicks sweat away from your body to keep you dry. Over that, add an insulating layer, like a fleece or a wool sweater, that will keep you warm. Your top layer should be a jacket that's both waterproof and breathable. It protects you from rain and wind but lets sweat escape.

Choosing the Right Fabrics - Cotton might be comfy, but it's not great for outdoor adventures. When it gets wet, it stays wet, which can make you cold. Instead, go for synthetic fabrics or wool. They dry quickly and keep you warm, even when they're damp. For pants, pick something sturdy but flexible. You need to move easily, whether you're climbing rocks or crossing streams.

Protect Your Head, Hands, and Feet - A lot of body heat is lost through your head, so wearing a hat is a must. It can be a warm hat for cold days or a sun hat to protect you from the sun. Gloves are essential too, especially if you're somewhere bristly or chilly. And let's not forget your feet. Good socks and shoes are your best friends on a hike. Go for socks that wick moisture away and shoes with a good grip that support your ankles.

Be Ready for the Sun - Even on cloudy days, the sun can be strong. A hat with a brim keeps the sun off your face, and sunglasses protect your eyes. Sunscreen is a must, no matter what the weather looks like.

Think Safety and Comfort - Bright colors are a good choice when you're outdoors. They make you easy to see, which is especially important if you're in a group or in an area with lots of people. Make sure your clothes aren't too tight or too loose. You should be able to move freely and comfortably.

Don't Forget the Extras - It's always good to pack an extra layer or two, just in case the weather changes. A lightweight, packable rain jacket can be a lifesaver if an unexpected rain shower comes up. And if you're going to be out from dawn till dusk, packing extra socks and a change of clothes is a good idea.

Dressing Smartly for Different Weathers - The way you dress changes with the weather. On hot days, light-colored, loose-fitting clothes help keep you cool. In colder weather, it's all about staying warm and dry. Waterproof and insulated gear is key. If it's windy, a wind-resistant layer will make a big difference. And in snowy conditions, waterproof boots and thermal layers are essential.

Accessorize Wisely - Accessories are more than just fashion statements; they're part of your survival kit. A bandana or a buff can protect your neck from the sun or keep you warm. A belt can be handy for hanging small tools. Even your watch is important — choose one that's tough and waterproof.

Practice Wearing Your Gear - Before you head out, try wearing your gear at home or on a short walk. Make sure everything fits well and feels comfortable. It's better to adjust your layers and gear before you're out on the trail.

Dressing for survival doesn't mean you can't be stylish. But it does mean choosing clothes and gear that will keep you safe, comfortable, and prepared for anything. Think of it as your adventure uniform, each piece chosen for a purpose, each item part of your story as an explorer. So, dress smart, pack right, and you're ready to face the great outdoors with confidence and style!

BE RESPECTFUL OF NATURE
(TAKE PHOTOS, LEAVE NOTHING)

Exploring the great outdoors is like visiting someone else's home. Just like you wouldn't leave trash on a friend's living room floor, it's important to show the same respect to nature. Being outdoors is a privilege, and with that comes the responsibility to take care of our natural world.

Leave No Trace - The rule is simple: leave no trace of your visit. This means whatever you bring in, you take back out. Trash, food wrappers, even things like fruit peels or seeds, shouldn't be left behind. They might seem harmless, but they can disrupt the natural environment. Animals might eat food that's not good for them, or non-native plants might start to grow.

Respect Wildlife - Wild animals are just that — wild. They're not like pets. Watching them from a distance is okay but getting too close can scare them and disrupt their natural behaviors. Feeding them can make them dependent on humans for food, which isn't healthy or safe for them. The best way to enjoy wildlife is to watch quietly and leave them undisturbed.

Stay on Trails - Trails are there for a reason. They guide you through the natural world while protecting fragile plants and ecosystems. Straying off the path can harm plant life and cause erosion. Sticking to trails ensures that the wilderness stays wild and beautiful for everyone to enjoy.

Take Only Photos, Leave Only Footprints - This old saying is the best rule of thumb. Take lots of photos to remember your adventure. But leave rocks, plants, and other natural objects where you find them. They're part of the ecosystem and removing them can cause damage. And of course, leave only footprints. This means not leaving any sign that you were there — no trash, no damage, just footprints that will soon be gone.

Campfire Care - If you're camping and making a campfire, be very careful. Only build fires in designated areas and make sure to put them out completely before you leave. A single spark can start a wildfire, so it's crucial to be cautious.

Use Eco-Friendly Gear - When you're choosing gear for your outdoor adventures, look for eco-friendly options. Things like biodegradable soap, reusable water bottles, and solar-powered chargers help reduce your environmental impact.

Respect Other Visitors - Remember, you're not the only one enjoying nature. Be courteous to other hikers and campers. Keep noise levels down, and don't disrupt others' experiences. Nature is a shared space, and everyone has a right to enjoy it peacefully.

Educate Yourself and Others - Learn about the places you visit. Understanding the local environment, the wildlife, and the challenges they face can help you appreciate and protect them. Share this knowledge with friends and family. The more people understand and respect nature, the better protected it will be.

Volunteer and Support Conservation Efforts - If you love being outdoors, consider giving back. Volunteer for clean-up days or support conservation groups. Your time and effort can make a big difference in preserving these natural spaces.

Being respectful of nature is about understanding our place in the world. We're just one part of a much larger ecosystem. Every action we take outdoors can have an impact, so it's important to make those actions positive. By being mindful and respectful, we can ensure that the beauty and wonder of nature will be there for generations to come. Enjoy the outdoors, treasure it, and most importantly, protect it.

TAKE ENOUGH WATER (MANY LIVE WITHOUT LOVE, NONE WITHOUT WATER)

Water is more than just a drink; it's a lifeline, especially when you're out on an adventure. The importance of water cannot be overstated — it keeps you going, keeps you healthy, and can be a game changer in the outdoors. Here's how you make sure you have enough water to turn your adventure into a success story.

Understand Your Water Needs - The amount of water you need depends on many factors — the weather, the intensity of your activity, and your own body. As a rule of thumb, you should drink about half a liter of water every hour during moderate activity in moderate weather. However, if it's hot or if you're doing something strenuous like hiking up a hill, you'll need more.

Carry Enough Water - Always carry more water than you think you'll need. It's better to have extra than to run out. A good practice is to take a big drink of water before you start your adventure and then fill up your water bottle or hydration pack. This way, you start off well-hydrated.

Know Where to Find Water - If you're going on a longer trip, research your water sources. Are there streams or lakes on your route? If so, you'll need a way to purify that water, because even the clearest mountain stream can have bacteria or viruses. Boiling water, water purification tablets, or a water filter are your go-tos for making sure your water is safe to drink.

Stay Hydrated, Stay Healthy - Staying hydrated keeps your body working like it should. It helps regulate your temperature, keeps your joints moving smoothly, and helps your brain stay sharp. When you're well-hydrated, you're more alert, more energetic, and in a better mood.

Recognize the Signs of Dehydration - Know the signs of dehydration. Feeling thirsty, having a dry mouth, feeling tired, or having a headache are early signs. If you notice any of these, it's time to take a water break.

Don't Wait Until You're Thirsty - Don't wait until you feel thirsty to drink water. Thirst is a sign that your body is already heading towards dehydration. Drink water regularly throughout your adventure.

Use Your Water Wisely - If you find yourself running low on water, use it wisely. Avoid activities that make you sweat a lot. Stay in the shade if it's hot. Plan your route so you can refill your water as soon as possible.

Teach Kids the Value of Water - For the little adventurers, it's crucial to teach them the value of water. Make sure they understand why it's important to drink water regularly and teach them to recognize the signs of needing a drink.

Be Mindful of the Environment - While you're taking care of yourself, take care of nature too. If you're using soap or toothpaste near a water source, make sure it's biodegradable. And always keep a safe distance from water sources to avoid contamination.

Water is the essence of life, and this is never truer than when you're out enjoying nature. By staying hydrated, you ensure that your adventure is as fun and safe as it can be. Keep your water bottle filled, drink regularly, and let the adventures roll!

CHAPTER 2

HOW TO FIND WATER

Water, our most important friend in the wild! Without it, we couldn't hike, play, or explore for long. But don't worry, finding water isn't as tough as finding a needle in a haystack. It's all about knowing where to look and how to make it safe to drink.

First things first, why is water so crucial? Our bodies are like spongy water balloons. We need water to think, walk, and even breathe. Without enough water, we start feeling like a dried-out leaf. So, keeping hydrated, which means drinking plenty of water, is like keeping our internal engine running smoothly.

Now, where do you find water in the wild? It's like a game of nature's hide and seek. Streams, rivers, and lakes are obvious spots, but there's more. Can you see birds flying in a line or animals walking on a path? Follow them! They often lead to water. And if you see green, lush plants, there's a good chance water isn't far away.

But wait! Before you take a sip, let's talk about making water safe. Drinking straight from a stream can be like eating unwashed fruit - not a good idea. Tiny things in water, too small to see, can make us sick. So, how do we outsmart them? Boiling water is one way. It's like giving the water a good, hot bath to chase away the germs. If you can't boil it, special tablets or filters work like magic, cleaning the water for you.

Here's a fun trick! If you can't find a stream, dig a hole near plants or in a muddy area. Often, water seeps into the hole, like a mini spring. Cover it with leaves to keep it clean and come back later to a small, secret water supply.

HYDRATION IS KEY: WHY WATER IS CRITICAL FOR WILDERNESS SURVIVAL

Water is the most important thing you need in the wild. It's more than just a drink; it's your body's best buddy, keeping you going when you're hiking, exploring, or just having fun outdoors. You might wonder, why is water so essential? Let's dive into this and find out.

Every part of your body, from your brain to your toes, needs water to work well. Without enough water, things start going wrong. You might feel tired, get a headache, or even feel dizzy. That's your body's way of saying, "Hey, I need water!" Think of water as fuel for a car. Without fuel, a car can't move. The same goes for your body without water.

Now, let's talk about sweat. When you're out playing or hiking, you sweat. Sweat is your body's air conditioning system, keeping you cool. But when you sweat, you're losing water. So, you need to drink more to fill up your body's water tank.

But how much water do you need? Well, it's not the same for everyone. It depends on how active you are and how hot it is outside. A good rule of thumb is to take small sips of water often, especially if you're running around or it's a sunny day.

Finding water in the wilderness can be tricky. But nature gives clues. Look for green areas with lots of plants; usually, water is nearby. Streams, rivers, and lakes are great, but remember, the water might not be clean. That's why it's important to know how to make water safe to drink.

Boiling water is one of the best ways to make it safe. When you boil water, it kills the tiny germs that can make you sick. If you can't boil water, there are other options like water purification tablets or filters. They are like superheroes, fighting off the bad germs in the water.

Sometimes, you might not find a stream or a lake. Don't worry; there's still a way to get water. You can collect rainwater or even use a piece of cloth to soak up dew from plants in the morning. Nature has a lot of hidden water sources!

Staying hydrated also means knowing the signs when you're not drinking enough. Feeling thirsty, tired, or having a dry mouth are signs that your body needs water. It's better to drink water before you feel these signs. Like a gardener waters plants before they wilt, you should drink water before you feel too thirsty.

In some situations, you might have to ration your water, which means using it carefully. If you have a limited amount of water, take small sips throughout the day instead of drinking a lot at once. This helps your body stay hydrated longer.

Lastly, always carry a water bottle when you're out in the wild. It's your personal water supply. And remember, while exploring, always think ahead. Know where you can find water and how to make it safe to drink. This way, you'll be prepared for any adventure that comes your way!

Water is not just a thirst quencher. It's a vital part of staying healthy and energetic, especially when you're out in nature. By understanding the importance of hydration and how to find and purify water in the wild, you're equipping yourself with crucial survival skills. So, next time you're gearing up for an outdoor adventure, remember to put water at the top of your list. Stay hydrated and explore the wonders of the wilderness with confidence and care!

HOW TO FIND WATER SOURCES IN THE WILD

Finding water in the wild is a bit like a treasure hunt. It's all about knowing where to look and how to spot the clues nature gives you. Let's explore the ways to find this precious liquid on your outdoor adventures.

Follow Nature's Lead - Animals and plants are great indicators of water nearby. Birds often fly towards water in the morning and evening. Animal tracks can also lead to water sources. Ants avoid water, so if you see them climbing high, water might be close. Bees can lead you to water too, as they need it to make honey.

Look at the Landscape - Valleys and low areas often collect water. If you're in a hilly or mountainous area, head downwards. Dry riverbeds or creek beds can also lead to water. Even if they're dry, digging in these areas can sometimes reveal water just below the surface.

Collect Rainwater - Rainwater is a clean source of water. You can collect it using any clean container or tarp. If you have a rain jacket or poncho, use it to funnel rainwater into a container.

Dew Collection - Early in the morning, dew forms on grass and leaves. You can collect dew by wiping it with a cloth and then wringing the water into a container. This method won't provide a lot of water, but every drop counts!

Use Plants - Some plants like the vine of the water vine or the stem of a banana or papaya tree contain drinkable water. Cut the vine or stem and collect the water that drips out. Be careful, though not all plants are safe to drink from.

Snow and Ice - If it's cold enough for snow and ice, melting it can provide water. But never eat snow directly as it lowers your body temperature. Melt it first.

Rock Creases and Crevices - Rocks can catch and hold water in their creases and crevices. Explore areas where rocks are abundant, and you might find small pools of water.

Solar Still - You can make a solar still with a plastic sheet, a container, and a digging tool. Dig a hole, place the container in the center, and cover the hole with the plastic sheet. Place a small stone in the center of the sheet above the container. Moisture from the ground and plants will condense on the plastic and drip into the container.

Safety First - Once you find water, remember, it needs to be purified before drinking. Boiling, filtering, or using purification tablets are your best bets. Never drink water that looks dirty or smells bad.

By learning to read the signs nature provides, you become a skilled water detective in the wild. Remember, water is everywhere; you just need to know where to look. With these tips, you'll never be far from a water source on your wilderness adventures.

METHODS OF WATER PURIFICATION

In the wild, finding water is only half the task; the other half is making it safe to drink. Purifying water means getting rid of the tiny, invisible things that could make you sick. Let's dive into the different ways to purify water, turning it from questionable to quenchable.

Boiling: The Heat is On - Boiling is one of the simplest and most effective methods to purify water. All you need is a fire and a pot. Once the water reaches a rolling boil, keep it boiling for about a minute. This heat zaps away harmful things in the water. If you're at a higher altitude, where water boils at a lower temperature, boil it for a bit longer.

Filtering: Through the Sieve - Water filters are like sieves that catch the bad stuff while letting the clean water through. There are many types of water filters: pump filters, straw filters, and gravity filters. Some use a hand pump to push water through a filter, while others let gravity do the work. Filters can get rid of bacteria and other nasties, but they might not catch everything, like viruses.

Chemical Purifiers: Tablet Teamwork - Chemical purifiers come in tablets or liquid form. These chemicals, usually iodine or chlorine, are added to the water. They work by killing bacteria and viruses. The catch? They need time to work, usually about 30 minutes, and they might leave a slight taste behind. If you're sensitive to the taste, a pinch of powdered drink mix can help mask it.

UV Light Purifiers: Sun's Little Helper - UV light purifiers use ultraviolet light to zap microbes in the water. These handy gadgets, often the size of a small flashlight, are swirled around in the water for a few minutes. The UV light scrambles the germs' DNA, stopping them from making you sick. They're effective but need batteries to work and might not be the best choice for cloudy or very dirty water.

Solar Disinfection: Bottle in the Sun - This method is as simple as filling a clear plastic bottle with water and leaving it out in the sun for about six hours. The UV rays from the sun work like the UV light purifier. It's a slow process and works best on sunny days. If the water is murky, it should be filtered through a cloth first.

Distillation: Steamy Solution - Distillation involves boiling water and then collecting the steam, which turns back into water. This method removes salt, metals, and other non-water particles. It's effective but requires a setup to capture steam, and it's not the quickest method.

Natural Purification: Mother Nature's Method - Sometimes, you can use natural materials to purify water. Sand, charcoal, and gravel can be layered in a bottle to make a simple filter. Pour water through the top and collect it as it drips out the bottom. This method can improve the clarity and taste of the water, but it's not as reliable for removing all harmful organisms.

Sedimentation: Letting it Settle - For very dirty water, let it sit undisturbed so that the heavy particles settle at the bottom. Then, you can gently pour off the clearer water on top and purify it using one of the other methods.

Each method has its pros and cons. Boiling and chemical purifiers are great all-rounders, while filters and UV purifiers are handy for on-the-go. Solar disinfection is simple but weather-dependent, and distillation is thorough but complex. Remember, no method is perfect on its own. Sometimes, combining methods, like filtering and then boiling, can give you the safest water.

In the wild, having clean water is as important as finding shelter or food. By knowing these purification methods, you can turn almost any water source into a safe, drinkable one. So next time you're out exploring, keep these techniques in mind, and you'll always stay hydrated and healthy on your adventures.

OTHER TIPS AND TRICKS TO FINDING WATER

In the great outdoor adventure, knowing how to find water is a skill as cool as being a detective. There are some neat tricks that can help you spot water even when it seems like there's none around. Let's uncover these secrets, so you're never thirsty on your wilderness explorations.

1. Morning Dew Magic. In the early morning, dew forms on grass and leaves. It's nature's way of making water. You can collect dew by gently wiping it off with a cloth and squeezing the water into a container. It might not fill a bottle, but every drop helps!

2. Fruitful Finds. Some fruits and plants hold water. Cacti or thick-leaved plants often store water. Be careful, though! Some plants can be tricky and not all are safe to drink from. It's best to learn about safe, water-storing plants before your trip.

3. Rock Hollows: Nature's Bowls. After a rain, look for hollows in rocks. These natural bowls can hold water. It's like finding small puddles just waiting to be discovered. But, always purify this water before drinking.

4. Rain Gear Reservoir. Your raincoat isn't just for staying dry. Spread it out during a rain shower and collect the water. It's a simple trick that can catch quite a bit of rainwater, especially during a heavy downpour.

5. Tree Tricks. Trees can be water finders, too. Tie a clean bag around a leafy tree branch. The water that the tree releases, called transpiration, collects at the bottom of the bag. By the end of the day, you might have enough for a sip or two.

6. Digging for Water. In dry streambeds or valleys, dig a hole. Water can seep into the hole from underground. This trick requires patience and a bit of luck. Make sure you dig in a place where water is likely to be, like a low-lying area.

7. Listening Skills. Sometimes, you can hear water before you see it. Listen for the sound of a stream or a river, especially in quiet, hilly areas. Water makes distinct sounds as it moves over rocks and through the land.

8. Watch the Wildlife. Animals need water just like humans. Birds often fly lower when near water. Animal tracks can also lead to water sources. Observing wildlife behavior can give you clues about where to find water.

9. Cloudy Clues. Clouds tend to form more easily over water. So, if you see clouds gathering or staying over a particular area, there might be a water source nearby.

10. Use Technology. If you're carrying a smartphone or a GPS device, they can be handy tools. Many apps and devices have maps that show nearby rivers, lakes, and other water sources. Just remember, technology can fail, so it's good to know these other tricks too.

11. Frost and Snow. In colder environments, melting snow or frost can give you water. Be sure to melt it first, as eating snow directly can lower your body temperature.

12. Safety First. Always remember, finding water is just the start. Making sure it's safe to drink is crucial. Boil, filter, or purify it to ensure you stay healthy on your outdoor adventure.

These tips and tricks are like keys to unlocking the secrets of finding water in the wild. They require a mix of observation, patience, and a bit of adventure spirit. With these skills in your adventure toolkit, you'll be ready to quench your thirst wherever your journeys take you. Remember, nature is full of surprises, and knowing how to find water is one of the coolest ways to be prepared for your outdoor explorations.

CHAPTER 3

SECURING OR
BUILDING A SHELTER

When you're out in the wild, your shelter is like your home away from home. It's not just a place to sleep; it's your safe spot, your fortress against the elements, and sometimes, a cozy haven for dreaming under the stars. Understanding how to find or create a shelter is like learning to build your own castle in nature.

There's a whole world of shelters to explore. From the simplicity of a bivouac sack (bivvy for short) — a small, lightweight shelter — to the sturdy reliability of a tent, each type has its own charm and purpose. Then there are the more adventurous kinds, like snow caves for the snowy terrains, or natural caves that have been nature's shelters for centuries.

Building your own shelter is an adventure in itself. It's about being resourceful, using what nature provides, and putting your creativity to work. It could be a lean-to made from branches, a hut with a roof of leaves, or even a more elaborate setup using tarps and ropes. Each step in building a DIY shelter teaches you about survival, resourcefulness, and the art of improvising.

But it's not just about building; it's also about choosing the right spot. The perfect location for your shelter is more than just a beautiful view. It's about safety, protection from wind and rain, and being aware of the surroundings. Is the ground dry and level? Are there any dangers like falling branches or rising water nearby? Picking the right spot can turn a good shelter into the perfect shelter.

Whether you're pitching a tent, rolling out a bivvy, or building your shelter from scratch, each experience enriches your adventure and teaches you valuable skills. So, let's dive into the exciting world of shelters, where every structure you build or choose becomes a part of your unforgettable outdoor journey.

TYPES OF SHELTERS (BIVVY, TENT, DIY, SNOW CAVE, NATURAL CAVES, ETC.)

When venturing into the great outdoors, one of the most exciting parts is where you'll stay. Different types of shelters suit different adventures, each with its own unique flair and purpose. From the snugness of a bivvy to the crafting of a DIY shelter, understanding these options can turn a night in the wilderness into an unforgettable experience.

Bivvy - The Compact Shelter - A bivouac sack, known as a bivvy, is the minimalist's dream. It's a small, lightweight shelter that's just big enough for one person to sleep in. Think of it as a waterproof, windproof bag for your sleeping bag. Bivvies are perfect for solo adventurers who want to travel light and fast. They're easy to set up and offer a snug place to rest while watching the stars.

Tents - The Classic Choice - Tents are the most common type of shelter for campers. They come in various sizes, from small two-person tents to large family-sized ones. Tents provide more space and comfort than bivvies and offer protection from insects and the elements. Setting up a tent is like creating your own little home in the wilderness. You can fill it with your sleeping bag, a pillow, and even a small lantern for a cozy night.

DIY Shelters - The Creative Approach - Building your own shelter can be a fun and rewarding challenge. Using materials like branches, leaves, tarps, and ropes, you can create a range of shelters, such as lean-tos or A-frames. These DIY shelters give you a sense of accomplishment and a deeper connection to the environment. They require creativity and some basic survival skills, making the building process an adventure in itself.

Snow Caves - The Winter Fortress - For snowy environments, snow caves offer a surprisingly warm and secure shelter. They are built by digging into deep snow and creating a space large enough to lie down in. The snow acts as an insulator, trapping your body heat inside. Building a snow cave takes effort and knowledge, but it's an essential skill for winter wilderness survival.

Natural Caves - Nature's Own Shelter - Sometimes, nature provides the shelter. Natural caves can be found in many wilderness areas. They offer protection from the wind and rain and require no setup. However, it's important to be cautious with natural caves. They can be home to animals or have loose rocks, so always inspect a cave carefully before deciding to use it as a shelter.

Hammocks - Sleeping Among the Trees - For those who love to be rocked to sleep, hammocks are an enticing option. Suspended between two sturdy trees, hammocks keep you off the ground and can be incredibly relaxing. They're ideal for warm, dry climates and offer a unique way to experience the outdoors.

Choosing Your Shelter - When picking a shelter, think about the environment you'll be in, the weather, and what you feel comfortable setting up. Each type of shelter offers different experiences and challenges. Whether it's the simplicity of a bivvy under the stars, the comfort of a tent, or the satisfaction of building your own shelter, your choice can make your outdoor adventure all the more special.

Remember, the shelter you choose is more than just a place to sleep. It's your basecamp for adventure, your protection from the wild, and your cozy corner in the vast outdoors. So choose wisely, set up carefully, and enjoy your time connecting with nature in your very own wilderness abode.

HOW TO BUILD A SURVIVAL SHELTER (STEP BY STEP DIY SHELTER)

In the heart of nature, building your own survival shelter can be an exciting and useful skill. Whether you're on an adventurous hike or find yourself in an unexpected situation, knowing how to construct a shelter with natural materials can be both empowering and lifesaving. Here's a step-by-step guide to creating a basic, yet effective, survival shelter.

Step 1: Find the Right Location. Location is everything. Look for a spot that's dry and flat. Avoid areas under large trees with loose branches, and stay clear of low spots that could fill with water. If you can, find a location near a water source, but not too close to avoid dampness or flooding.

Step 2: Gather Materials. You'll need two main types of materials: something for the frame (like long, sturdy sticks) and something for the covering (like leaves, grass, or moss). Look for fallen branches and twigs — no need to damage living trees.

Step 3: Construct the Frame. Start by finding a long, sturdy branch to be the ridgepole — the backbone of your shelter. Place one end on the ground and the other on a tree stump or forked branches. Then, lean shorter branches against the ridgepole on both sides, creating a frame that looks like an A-frame tent.

Step 4: Insulate and Cover. Once your frame is in place, it's time to insulate. Start from the bottom and work your way up, layering leaves, grass, or moss. The idea is to create a thick, dense cover that can block wind and rain. Make sure you cover the sides and the back.

Step 5: Create an Entrance. Leave a space at one end of the A-frame as an entrance. You can partially cover this with more branches to keep it sheltered yet accessible.

Step 6: Reinforce Your Shelter. Add extra branches, vines, or bark to secure the covering materials. Make sure everything is tightly packed and stable. The more secure your shelter, the better it will protect you from the elements.

Step 7: Build a Bed. Inside your shelter, build a bed to keep you off the ground. Use dry leaves, grass, or pine needles. This bed acts as insulation, keeping you warmer through the night.

Step 8: Test Your Shelter. Once your shelter is built, it's a good idea to test its sturdiness. Gently push against the sides and the ridgepole to make sure everything holds. Check for any gaps in the covering and fill them in as needed.

Step 9: Customize as Needed. Depending on the materials available and the weather conditions, you might need to customize your shelter. In colder weather, make the walls thicker. If it's windy, make sure the entrance is facing away from the wind.

Step 10: Maintain Your Shelter. Your shelter might need maintenance, especially if you're using it for more than one night. Check regularly for any weak spots or holes and repair them as needed.

Building a survival shelter is more than just a survival skill. It's a lesson in resourcefulness, adaptability, and connection with the natural world. It teaches patience, problem-solving, and respect for nature. Each step in building your shelter brings you closer to understanding the environment and how to live harmoniously within it.

WHICH TENT SHOULD I BUY?
(KEY FACTORS TO CONSIDER IN TENT SELECTION)

Choosing the right tent for your outdoor adventures can be like picking a new house. It's going to be your shelter, your safe space in the wild, and your cozy corner under the stars. But with so many tents out there, how do you pick the perfect one? Here's what you need to think about to make a smart choice.

1. Size and Space. First, think about how much space you need. Tents are often labeled by the number of people they can sleep. But remember, a two-person tent means it can fit two people side by side, usually without much extra room. If you want space for your backpack, or if you like a bit more elbow room, consider sizing up.

2. Weight. If you're backpacking, the weight of the tent is crucial. A heavy tent can weigh you down on long hikes. Look for tents labeled as 'backpacking tents' — they're designed to be lightweight and easy to carry. If you're camping close to your car, weight isn't as much of a concern, so you can go for something a bit heavier with more features.

3. Season Rating. Tents come with season ratings — 2-season, 3-season, and 4-season. A 2-season tent is good for mild weather and minimal rain. A 3-season tent is the most popular; it's designed for spring, summer, and fall, can handle rain, and has good ventilation. A 4-season tent is built for serious winter conditions — it's stronger, with less ventilation, designed to keep you warm and withstand snow and strong winds.

4. Ease of Setup. Look for a tent that's easy to set up. After a long day of hiking, you don't want to spend hours fighting with tent poles. Some tents pop up on their own, while others might take a bit of practice. It's always a good idea to do a test run at home before you take your tent into the wild.

5. Material and Durability. Check what the tent is made of. The material should be durable and waterproof. The floor of the tent, known as the footprint, should be tough enough to handle rough ground. Zippers need to be sturdy and snag-free. Remember, a good tent is an investment that should last you many adventures.

6. Ventilation. Proper ventilation is key to staying comfortable in a tent. Look for tents with mesh panels or windows. These help keep condensation down and reduce the stuffiness inside a tent, especially on warm nights.

7. Price. Tents come in a wide range of prices. While it's tempting to go for the cheapest option, it might not always be the best choice in the long run. Investing in a good quality tent means it'll last longer and stand up better to the elements. However, there are plenty of mid-range options that offer a good balance between quality and price.

8. Extra Features. Consider the extra features. Does it have enough pockets for your gear? What about a vestibule for your muddy boots? Maybe you want a lantern hook for night-time reading. These little things can make a big difference in your camping experience.

9. Read Reviews and Ask Around. Before making a decision, read reviews and ask other campers for their recommendations. Sometimes the best advice comes from those who have tested their tents in the wild.

Selecting the right tent is about balancing your needs with the right features. Think about where you'll be camping, what the weather will be like, and what comforts you need. A good tent is like a trusty companion on your outdoor adventures — reliable, cozy, and always there to give you a home wherever you may wander.

LOCATION, LOCATION, LOCATION (WHERE TO SAFELY PUT A SHELTER?)

Finding the perfect spot to set up your shelter is a bit like being a detective. It's not just about finding a place that looks nice; it's about finding a spot that will keep you safe, comfortable, and protected throughout your stay in the wild. Here's what you need to look for when choosing the ideal location for your shelter.

1. Flat Ground. Start by looking for flat ground. It's more comfortable for sleeping, and it's easier to set up your shelter on a level surface. An uneven or sloped area can make your night restless and could even send you sliding down in your sleep.

2. Dry Land. Avoid low-lying areas that could collect rainwater and become damp or flooded. Look for slightly elevated areas where water is less likely to pool. But don't go too high — the top of a hill can be exposed to strong winds.

3. Shelter from the Wind. A good shelter spot is one that's protected from the wind. Look for natural windbreakers like bushes, trees, or rocks. However, be cautious about setting up right under trees — falling branches can be a hazard, especially in windy or stormy weather.

4. Safe Distance from Water Sources. While being near a water source is convenient, setting up too close can be risky. Rivers or lakes can rise unexpectedly, and areas near water often attract wildlife. A safe distance ensures you stay dry and less likely to have animal visitors.

5. Be Aware of Wildlife. Speaking of animals, consider the wildlife in the area. Avoid places that look like animal paths or areas with signs of animal activity like nests or droppings. Keeping a respectful distance from wildlife keeps both you and the animals safe.

6. Look Up and Around. Always look up and around the area. Check for loose rocks, dead branches, or unstable terrain. These could be dangerous in windy conditions or if disturbed.

7. Consider the Sun. Think about where the sun will rise and set. East-facing locations get morning sun, which can be pleasant on a chilly morning. However, in very hot weather, a spot that's shaded in the afternoon can be a lifesaver.

8. Respect Nature and Regulations. Choose a spot that has the least impact on the surrounding environment. Stick to designated camping areas or previously used spots. Make sure to follow any local rules or regulations about where you can set up shelter.

9. Access to Emergency Exits. Consider your access to emergency exits or pathways. You should know how to quickly and safely leave your campsite if needed. This is especially important in areas prone to natural hazards like wildfires or floods.

10. Personal Preference. Lastly, think about what you want from your camping experience. Do you want to be near a beautiful view for the sunrise? Or maybe you prefer being close to a trailhead for an early start on your hike. Personal preference plays a big role in choosing your spot.

Finding the right location for your shelter is a crucial part of your outdoor adventure. It's about balancing comfort, safety, and respect for the environment. Take your time to assess the area, think about these factors, and choose a spot that will turn your outdoor stay into a delightful and memorable experience. Remember, a great location not only provides safety but also adds to the joy of being immersed in the natural world.

CHAPTER 4

HOW TO MAKE A FIRE

Mastering the art of fire-making is like unlocking a secret power of the wilderness. A fire is more than just a source of warmth; it's a beacon in the night, a cozy gathering place, and a vital tool for cooking. When you're out in the wild, knowing how to make a fire can make all the difference. It's a skill that connects us with our ancestors, who long ago learned to harness this element for survival and comfort.

Starting a fire is both a science and an art. It requires patience, the right materials, and a bit of know-how. From gathering dry twigs and leaves to arranging them just right, every step is important. You'll learn to read the environment, choosing the best spot for your fire, where it's sheltered from the wind but still safe and away from too many dry leaves or branches.

This chapter is all about the basics of fire-making. You'll discover various techniques to start a fire, from the traditional use of sticks and stones to the more modern methods like matches or a firestarter. It's fascinating how with just a spark, you can bring warmth and light to the wilderness.

But it's not just about starting a fire. You'll also dive into how to find the best natural materials for keeping your fire going. Different weather conditions, like rain or wind, bring their own challenges, and you'll learn how to build and maintain a fire in these situations.

Safety is key. A fire is a powerful tool, and with great power comes great responsibility. You'll learn how to keep your fire under control, how to put it out properly, and leave no trace, ensuring the safety of the wilderness and its inhabitants.

TECHNIQUES FOR STARTING A FIRE

The art of fire-making is a cornerstone of wilderness skills. It's a blend of knowledge, practice, and a bit of patience. In this part, we'll explore various techniques to start a fire, helping you become a proficient fire-maker, ready for your outdoor adventures.

Finding the Right Spot - Choosing the right location for your fire is crucial. Look for a spot that's sheltered from the wind, away from trees and bushes. Clear the ground of dry leaves and twigs, creating a bare earth circle. This helps prevent the fire from spreading.

Gathering Materials - A good fire starts with the right materials. You'll need three types: tinder, kindling, and fuel wood. Tinder is material that catches fire easily, like dry grass, leaves, or small twigs. Kindling is slightly larger and helps the fire grow, like sticks as thick as a pencil. Fuel wood keeps the fire going, and these are larger pieces of wood.

Traditional Methods: Friction-Based Fires - One of the oldest fire-making methods uses friction. The most common techniques are the hand drill and the bow drill. The hand drill involves spinning a stick between your hands, pressing it into a base wood piece with a notch. The bow drill is similar but uses a bow to spin the stick more efficiently. Both methods create heat from friction, eventually producing an ember that can ignite your tinder.

Modern Methods: Matches and Lighters - Matches and lighters are the most convenient methods to start a fire. Always keep them dry. Waterproof matches or a reliable lighter are great additions to your outdoor kit.

Using a Firestarter - Firestarters can be commercial products or homemade ones. Simple homemade firestarters can be made from items like cotton balls dipped in petroleum jelly. They catch fire easily and burn long enough to ignite kindling.

Magnifying Glass: Using the Sun - On a sunny day, a magnifying glass can start a fire. Angle the glass to focus a beam of sunlight onto your tinder until it smokes and ignites. It's a slow process but fascinating and effective.

Creating a Spark: Flint and Steel - Flint and steel is another traditional method. Striking steel against flint produces sparks. Aim these sparks onto your tinder to ignite it. It requires practice but works even when wet.

Building Your Fire Structure - Once you have an ember or a small flame from your chosen method, carefully add it to your tinder. Gently blow or fan it to provide oxygen, helping the fire grow. Add kindling and then fuel wood, gradually increasing the size of the wood as the fire builds.

Safety and Responsibility - Remember, fire safety is paramount. Keep water or dirt nearby to extinguish the fire if needed. Never leave a fire unattended, and make sure it's completely out before leaving the site.

Practice Makes Perfect - Becoming skilled at fire-making takes practice. Try different methods and materials to see what works best for you. Understand that not every attempt will be successful, and that's okay. Each attempt teaches you something new.

Starting a fire is more than just a survival skill; it's a way to connect with a fundamental force of nature. It teaches respect for the environment and the importance of being prepared and responsible. With these techniques and a bit of practice, you'll be ready to light a fire that can cook your meals, warm your nights, and create lasting memories under the stars.

NATURAL FIRE STARTERS

In the heart of the wilderness, where modern conveniences are miles away, nature provides everything needed to start a fire. This section delves into the art of finding and using natural materials as fire starters, turning what the wild offers into the spark that ignites a warm, crackling fire.

Understanding Natural Tinder - The first step in fire-making is finding tinder, materials that catch fire easily and burn quickly. Ideal natural tinders are dry, light, and airy. Here are some common types:

- **Dry Grass and Leaves** - These are often the easiest to find. Ensure they are completely dry. Bundle them loosely to allow air to circulate, aiding in ignition.

- **Birch Bark**: - This bark peels off easily and is full of natural oils, making it an excellent fire starter. Even when damp, its oils help it catch fire.

- **Pine Resin** - Found in pine trees, resin is a sticky substance that burns hot and long. Look for areas where the tree sap has hardened or where it's seeping out of the tree.

- **Dry Pine Needles** - Pine needles, when dry, catch fire quickly. Gather a small bundle as part of your tinder.

- **Cattail Fluff** - Often found near water sources, the fluffy part of a cattail head ignites easily, making a great tinder.

- **Old Man's Beard (Usnea)** - This lichen hangs from tree branches and looks like a beard. It's a superb tinder, especially in damp environments.

Kindling: The Next Step - After tinder, kindling is essential to grow your fire. Kindling should be slightly larger than tinder, like small twigs and sticks, and as dry as possible.

- **Small Twigs and Sticks** - Look for these on the ground near trees. Avoid breaking twigs off living trees as they're often too moist.

- **Split Wood** - If you have larger pieces of wood, splitting them exposes the dry inside, which makes excellent kindling.

- **Fuel Wood: Keeping the Fire Going** - Once your fire is lit, you'll need fuel wood to keep it burning. Look for dead, dry wood. Fallen branches or logs work well. Remember, the dryer the wood, the better it will burn.

Creating a Fire Lay - With your tinder, kindling, and fuel wood gathered, it's time to build your fire lay. Start with your tinder bundle, then add kindling in a teepee or lean-to structure around it. Leave an opening to light the tinder and to allow air to flow. Gradually add larger pieces of kindling and then your fuel wood, building up the fire as it grows.

Tips for Success

- Always gather more tinder, kindling, and fuel wood than you think you'll need. Running out mid-fire-starting can be frustrating.

- Ensure everything is dry. Moisture is the enemy of fire-making.

- Be patient. Sometimes fire-making takes time and multiple attempts, especially in challenging conditions.

Safety and Leave No Trace - As you embrace the role of a fire maker, remember your responsibility to nature. Always create fires in designated areas or existing fire rings. Keep water or soil nearby to extinguish the fire. When you're done, make sure the fire is completely out and the area is as you found it.

The skill of using natural materials to start a fire connects us with the land and our ancestors. It's a practice of patience, respect for nature, and resourcefulness. As you learn to identify and use these natural fire starters, you'll not only be prepared for your wilderness adventures but also gain a deeper appreciation for the natural world around you.

FIRE-BUILDING STRUCTURES

Creating a fire isn't just about sparking a flame. It's also about shaping that flame to suit different needs, whether it's for cooking, warmth, or signaling. Each purpose calls for a unique fire structure. Knowing how to build these structures is a vital part of wilderness survival.

Teepee Fire: The Classic - The teepee fire is the most recognized structure. It's ideal for warmth and can be used for cooking too. To build a teepee fire:

1. Place your tinder bundle in the center of your cleared space.

2. Arrange kindling sticks around it, leaning them against each other to form a teepee shape.

3. Gradually add larger sticks, still maintaining the teepee shape.

4. Leave an opening to light the tinder and for air to flow. This structure allows air to circulate freely, feeding the fire and creating a strong flame.

Log Cabin Fire: Stable and Long-Lasting - A log cabin fire is great for cooking and provides steady, lasting warmth. It's built like a log cabin, with layers of logs or sticks.

1. Start with a small teepee fire in the center.

2. Around this, lay your first layer of larger sticks or logs, parallel to each other on opposite sides of the teepee.

3. Add another layer perpendicular to the first.

4. Continue adding layers, reducing the size as you build up. This structure creates a bed of hot coals, perfect for placing pots and pans on top for cooking.

Lean-To Fire: Quick and Effective - The lean-to fire is quick to build and effective in windy conditions.

1. Drive a long stick into the ground at a 30-degree angle, pointing into the wind.

2. Place your tinder underneath this stick.

3. Lean kindling sticks against the long stick, over the tinder.

4. Add more layers of kindling, followed by larger wood. The design protects the fire from the wind, directing the heat to a specific area.

Star Fire: Efficient Fuel Usage - The star fire, also known as the Indian fire, is efficient in fuel usage.

1. Lay five or six large logs or sticks in a star shape, with one end of each log meeting in the center where your tinder will be.

2. Light the tinder, and as it burns, push the logs inward gradually. This structure is ideal for a long-lasting fire without needing a lot of wood.

Platform Fire: For Wet Ground - When the ground is wet, a platform fire is your best bet.

1. Lay a foundation of green logs or stones to create a platform above the wet ground.

2. Build a teepee or log cabin fire structure on top of this platform. This keeps your fire off the damp ground and allows it to burn more efficiently.

Signal Fire: For Emergencies - In case of emergencies, a signal fire can be a lifesaver.

1. Build a large and tall teepee structure.

2. Add green branches or leaves on top to create more smoke.

3. Have a clear area around the fire to prevent it from spreading. These fires produce a lot of smoke, making them visible from a distance.

Safety First - No matter which fire structure you build, always prioritize safety.

- Keep water or soil nearby to extinguish the fire if necessary.

- Never leave your fire unattended.

- Make sure the fire is completely out before leaving the area.

Each fire structure serves a specific purpose and mastering these designs enhances your skills as a proficient outdoors person. Whether you're cooking a meal, staying warm on a chilly night, or in need of rescue, knowing how to build these fire structures can greatly improve your outdoor experience. With practice, you'll learn which structure works best for each situation, making you a versatile and responsible fire-maker.

WEATHER CONSIDERATIONS

Starting and maintaining a fire can feel like a thrilling challenge, especially when the weather adds its own twist. Different weather conditions, be it rain, wind, or snow, require special techniques and a bit of ingenuity. Understanding how to manage these conditions can turn you into a fire-making expert, ready for any outdoor adventure.

In the Rain - Making a fire in the rain might seem impossible, but it's doable with the right approach.

1. **Find Shelter**: First, find or create a sheltered spot. This could be under a large tree, a rock overhang, or a makeshift shelter.

2. **Use Dry Wood**: Look for dry wood under dense trees or gather wood before the rain starts. You can also split logs to reach the drier wood inside.

3. **Elevate Your Fire**: Build your fire on a raised platform, like a bed of rocks or a thick layer of branches, to avoid the wet ground.

4. **Protect Your Fire**: Use a tarp or a large piece of bark to shield your fire from falling rain, being careful not to cover it completely as fire needs air to breathe.

In the Wind - Wind can be both a friend and a foe when building a fire.

1. **Find a Windbreak**: Look for natural windbreakers like rocks, trees, or a hillside. You can also create a barrier using a backpack or other gear.

2. **Direction Matters**: Position your fire so the wind is blowing into the side of your fire structure, not directly into or away from it. This helps control the spread of the flames.

3. **Use the Lean-To Method**: Building a lean-to fire provides a shield against the wind while allowing enough air to feed the flames.

In the Snow - Snowy conditions require a solid foundation and insulation.

1. **Create a Platform**: Pack down the snow or build a platform with logs to prevent your fire from sinking.

2. **Use Evergreen Boughs**: Place evergreen boughs under your fire area to insulate it from the cold ground.

3. **Find Dry Wood**: Use dead branches from lower parts of trees, as they're more likely to be dry. You might need to dig through the snow to find usable wood.

General Tips for All Weather Conditions

- **Gather More Wood Than You Think You Need**: Weather can make fire maintenance more challenging, so having extra wood is always a good idea.

- **Protect Your Tinder and Kindling**: Keep your tinder and kindling dry by storing them in your jacket or under a shelter.

- **Use Fire Starters**: In challenging conditions, fire starters like wax, lint, or commercial starters can give you an edge.

Safety and Responsibility No matter the weather, fire safety is crucial. Always be aware of your surroundings and any potential risks. Keep water or soil nearby to extinguish the fire if needed, and ensure the fire is completely out before leaving the area.

Weather can be unpredictable, but with these techniques, you can master the art of fire-making in any condition. It's a skill that not only brings warmth and comfort but also a deep sense of achievement and connection with the natural world. Whether under a clear sky, amidst a gentle rain, or surrounded by snowflakes, your fire-making skills will light up your wilderness experience.

EXTINGUISHING AND LEAVING NO TRACE

After enjoying the warmth and light of a campfire, it's crucial to put it out safely and responsibly. Properly extinguishing a fire ensures the safety of the wilderness and its inhabitants. It's a practice in mindfulness and care for nature, leaving no trace of your presence.

The Right Way to Extinguish a Fire

1. **Start Early**: Don't wait until the last minute to put out your fire. Begin the process well before you plan to leave or sleep.

2. **Sprinkle Water**: Slowly sprinkle water over the fire. Don't pour it all at once, as this can create a cloud of ash and may not extinguish all embers.

3. **Stir the Ashes**: Use a stick or shovel to stir the ashes. This helps cool the fire faster and ensures all embers get wet.

4. **Check for Heat**: After you've sprinkled water and stirred the ashes, carefully feel for heat with the back of your hand near the ashes. Do not touch them directly.

5. **Add More Water if Necessary**: If you still feel heat, sprinkle more water and stir again. Repeat until the ashes are cool to the touch.

6. **Dispose of Charred Wood**: If there are charred logs or sticks that haven't burned completely, scatter them in a natural area away from the campsite.

Leaving No Trace

1. **Restore the Area**: Once the fire is out and cool, return the site to its natural state. If you built a fire ring, dismantle it and scatter the stones.

2. **Cover the Area**: Use local materials like leaves, soil, or sand to cover the area where the fire was. This helps the site recover and erases signs of your fire.

3. **Take Everything with You**: Ensure you leave nothing behind. This includes any trash or unused firewood. Pack everything out to preserve the natural beauty of the area.

Safety and Environmental Care

1. **Prevent Forest Fires**: By thoroughly extinguishing your fire, you help prevent forest fires, which can cause widespread damage to the environment and wildlife.

2. **Respect Wildlife**: A properly extinguished fire means animals can safely return to their habitat without the risk of injury or habitat loss.

3. **Maintain Clean Air and Water**: Ensuring that fires are completely out contributes to cleaner air and prevents ash from entering water sources.

The Importance of Responsibility Properly putting out a fire is more than a task; it's a responsibility. It's about caring for the environment and ensuring that the wild remains a safe and beautiful place for everyone and every creature that calls it home. Every time you put out a fire completely and leave no trace, you're taking an active part in preserving the natural world.

Whether you're a seasoned camper or a beginner in wilderness adventures, mastering the art of extinguishing a fire and leaving no trace is essential. It's a testament to your respect for nature and your commitment to preserving it for future generations. Remember, each of us plays a part in caring for our planet, and how we manage our fires is a significant part of that care.

STAY SAFE AND PROTECT THE ENVIRONMENT

Ensuring safety and respecting nature are two pillars of responsible fire-making in the wild. It's about being aware and considerate, not just for our well-being but for the health of the environment around us. This balance is key to a sustainable and enjoyable outdoor experience.

Understanding Fire Safety

1. **Choose the Right Spot**: Always make a fire in a designated area or a safe spot far from trees, bushes, and grass. Look for clearings or existing fire pits.

2. **Keep Fires Manageable**: Smaller fires are easier to control and extinguish. They also minimize the impact on the environment.

3. **Always Attend to Your Fire**: Never leave your fire unattended. A breeze can quickly turn a small fire into a dangerous one.

4. **Have Water and Tools Ready**: Always have water, sand, and a shovel nearby. These can be crucial if you need to put the fire out quickly.

5. **Teach and Practice Safety**: If you're with others, especially children, teach them the importance of fire safety. Practice what to do in case the fire gets out of control.

Protecting the Environment

1. **Use Existing Fire Rings**: If there's an existing fire ring or pit, use it. Creating new ones can damage the soil and plants.

2. **Gather Wood Responsibly**: Use only fallen branches or driftwood. Avoid breaking branches from living trees, as this harms the tree and the ecosystem.

3. **Avoid Damaging the Soil**: Building fires on the same spot repeatedly can sterilize the soil. Rotate fire spots if you're camping in one area for a long time.

4. **Be Cautious with Wildlife**: Keep your campfire area clean. Leftover food or scraps can attract wildlife, which can be dangerous for both you and the animals.

Leaving No Trace

1. **Erase Signs of Your Fire**: Once your fire is completely out and cool, scatter the ashes and restore the area.

2. **Carry Out What You Carry In**: Whatever you bring, take it back with you. This includes matches, wrappers, and any leftover wood.

3. **Naturalize the Area**: Leave the site as you found it or better. This helps preserve the natural beauty and integrity of the environment.

Being a Responsible Camper

1. **Understand Local Regulations**: Different areas have different rules regarding fires. Always check and follow local guidelines and fire bans.

2. **Consider Alternatives to Campfires**: In areas where fires are not recommended or are illegal, use a camping stove or enjoy the natural night without a fire.

3. **Educate Others**: Share your knowledge about fire safety and environmental care with fellow campers. Responsible practices grow through shared understanding and actions.

Ensuring safety and respecting nature go hand-in-hand when building and managing a fire. These practices protect not only the immediate surroundings but also the wider environment. By being cautious, mindful, and respectful, we can enjoy the primal allure of a campfire without harming the natural world we cherish and enjoy. This responsible approach to fire-making allows us to be guardians of the wilderness, ensuring its beauty and health for years to come.

CHAPTER 5

LOOKING FOR FOOD

In the great outdoors, finding food is an adventure all on its own. It's about connecting with nature in its purest form, understanding the rhythm of the wild, and tapping into ancient skills. This chapter is a guide to finding, identifying, and preparing food in the wilderness, a crucial skill for any outdoor enthusiast.

The art of foraging takes you into the heart of nature's pantry. Edible plants, fruits, and even insects can provide nourishment and energy. But it's not just about picking what looks good; it's about knowing what's safe to eat and what to avoid. With the right knowledge, the natural world opens up a buffet of options.

Seasons play a big role in what's available. Spring might offer tender greens and blossoms, summer brings berries and fruits, while fall is the time for nuts and seeds. Each season has its bounty, and knowing what to look for and when can turn foraging into a fruitful quest.

Safety is paramount in foraging. Not all plants are friendly, and some are downright dangerous. Learning to distinguish between edible and toxic plants is a vital skill. It's not just about what you pick, but also where you pick it. Avoiding areas that might be polluted or treated with chemicals is just as important.

For the more adventurous, there's the world of edible insects — a surprising source of protein and nutrients. And for those who are interested, an introduction to the basics of hunting and trapping provides insights into this age-old practice.

Lastly, knowing how to cook and prepare your wild finds is essential. With minimal equipment and a bit of creativity, you can turn nature's offerings into satisfying meals.

Embark on this journey of discovery and learn the skills to sustain yourself from the land. This chapter is not just about survival; it's about deepening your connection with the environment and understanding the delicate balance of nature. Whether you're foraging for berries or preparing a wild meal, you're participating in an age-old dance with nature, one that nourishes both the body and the spirit.

FORAGING WITH CARE

Foraging is like a treasure hunt in nature, where the prizes are edible plants and fruits. It's a skill that lets you explore the natural world and find food just as people have done for thousands of years. This section will guide you through the exciting world of foraging, focusing on how to identify what's edible and enjoy the bounty of nature safely.

Knowing What to Look For

- **Leafy Greens**: Many wild plants with green leaves are edible. Look for dandelion greens, lamb's quarters, and plantain leaves. These are often found in fields and alongside paths.
- **Berries**: Wild berries are a delicious find but be cautious. Learn to identify safe berries like blackberries, raspberries, and blueberries. Avoid white or yellow berries, as many are not safe to eat.
- **Nuts and Seeds**: Acorns, pine nuts, and sunflower seeds are some examples of edible nuts and seeds. Remember, nuts often need preparation like roasting or soaking.

Where to Forage

- **Forests and Woodlands**: These areas are great for mushrooms, berries, and nuts. Always be sure of mushroom identification, as some are very dangerous.
- **Fields and Open Areas**: Look here for leafy greens and wildflowers. Many wildflowers have edible petals.
- **Near Water Bodies**: Riversides and lakeshores can be good spots for cattails and watercress.

Safety First

- **Avoid Toxic Plants**: Some plants look edible but are toxic. Learn to identify plants like poison ivy, poison oak, and hemlock.

- **Use a Guidebook**: A good plant identification guidebook or an app can be a helpful tool. When in doubt, don't eat it.
- **Be Aware of Pesticides and Pollutants**: Avoid foraging near roadsides or areas that might be sprayed with chemicals.

Respecting Nature

- **Take Only What You Need**: Foraging is about being part of nature, not taking too much from it.
- **Leave No Trace**: Be careful not to damage the plants or the area around them.
- **Follow Local Rules**: Some areas have rules about foraging. Always follow these to protect the environment and local wildlife.

Preparing Your Finds

- **Wash Thoroughly**: Always wash your foraged food in clean water.
- **Cook if Necessary**: Some plants are more digestible when cooked. Simple cooking methods like boiling or steaming can be enough.

Learning and Sharing

- **Join Foraging Walks**: Many communities have guided foraging walks where you can learn from experts.
- **Share Knowledge Responsibly**: Teach others about safe foraging, but make sure your information is accurate.

Foraging is not just about finding food; it's about connecting with nature and understanding the ecosystem around you. It's a journey that enhances your appreciation of the outdoors, teaching you to see the land as a provider. With care and respect, foraging can be a rewarding adventure, filled with fresh flavors and the joy of discovery.

SEASONAL FORAGING: NATURE'S CALENDAR

Learning to forage through the seasons is not just about finding food; it's a journey through the year, discovering and connecting with the cycles of nature. This section unfolds the secrets of seasonal foraging, a skill that can bring joy and a sense of achievement.

Spring: The Awakening As winter's blanket thaws, nature stirs to life. Spring is a time of renewal, and the foraging treasures are fresh and vibrant.

Wild Greens: Plants like dandelion, nettles, and wild garlic emerge. These greens are not just delicious but are packed with nutrients.

Edible Flowers: Look for blossoms like violets and daisies. They add color and flavor to salads.

Tree Buds: Certain tree buds, like those of the beech tree, are edible and offer a soft, sweet taste.

Summer: The Abundant Season Summer's warmth brings an abundance of foraging options.

Berries: This is the time for berries - blackberries, raspberries, strawberries, and more. They're perfect for fresh eating, jams, and desserts.

Fruits: Wild fruits like cherries and plums can be found in woods and along hedgerows.

Herbs: Many herbs, such as mint and rosemary, are at their peak and great for flavoring dishes.

Autumn: The Harvest Autumn is a season of rich colors and bountiful harvest.

Nuts: Hazelnuts, chestnuts, and acorns are ready for collection. They require some preparation but are worth the effort.

Seeds: Pumpkin and sunflower seeds are not only edible but highly nutritious.

Late Berries: Look for late-season berries like elderberries, perfect for syrups and pies.

Winter: The Subtle Hunt While foraging in winter can be challenging, it's not impossible.

Roots: Roots like burdock and wild carrots can be dug up. They're great in soups and stews.

Evergreens: Some evergreen plants, like pine, have edible needles rich in vitamin C.

Foraging Safely Through the Seasons

Know What You're Picking: Misidentification can lead to picking toxic plants. Use a good guidebook or join a local foraging group.

Respect the Environment: Take only what you need and leave no trace of your foraging.

Prepare Properly: Learn how to clean and cook your finds. Some plants need special preparation to be edible.

Stories from the Field

Emma's Berry Adventure: At 16, Emma discovered the joy of picking wild berries. She learned to make jams that her family loved, turning her summer foraging into a delicious tradition.

Jason's Nut Foraging: Jason, a 14-year-old nature enthusiast, started foraging for nuts in autumn. He learned to roast chestnuts and even tried making acorn flour, exploring the flavors of the season.

Balancing the Bounty: While success stories like Emma's and Jason's inspire, it's also about the journey. It's about the sunny afternoons spent wandering through nature, the quiet satisfaction of preparing a meal with your finds, and the knowledge gained with each outing.

Foraging Through the Seasons: A Lifelong Skill: Seasonal foraging is more than a hobby; it's a skill that connects you with nature's rhythm. It teaches patience, respect for the environment, and offers a way to understand the land. As you move through the seasons, you'll not only find food but also a deeper connection to the world around you.

In a world where everything is available at the click of a button, foraging is a reminder of nature's pace and bounty. It's a skill that nurtures not just our bodies but our spirits, reminding us of the simple joys and wonders of nature. So, grab a basket and step outside; the wild is waiting with its seasonal offerings, ready to be discovered and savored.

SAFE FORAGING PRACTICES

Foraging is like a game of exploration in nature's backyard, where the greens, berries, and nuts you find are the hidden treasures. However, like any adventure, it comes with rules to keep you safe and make sure the game is fun and rewarding. In this chapter, we'll learn how to forage safely, making sure we only pick the good stuff and steer clear of any toxic tricksters. Ready to become a super safe foraging specialist? Let's dive in!

The Golden Rules of Foraging

- **Know Before You Nibble:** Always, always make sure you can positively identify a plant before you decide to taste it. Some plants have look-alikes that are not so friendly. Use a guidebook, or better yet, learn from an experienced forager.

- **When in Doubt, Go Without:** If you're not 100% sure, don't eat it! It's not worth the tummy trouble or a trip to the doctor. Our motto is "doubt means don't!"

- **Tiny Tastes:** If you're sure a plant is safe and an adult says it's okay, try just a small bit first. Wait to see how your body feels. Some people might be allergic to foods that are safe for others.

- **Clean Cuisine:** Wash all wild foods before you eat them. You don't want a side of dirt or little critters with your meal, do you?

- **Permission Patrol:** Only forage in places where it's allowed. Some areas protect their plants, and we want to respect that. Plus, no foraging in someone's backyard without asking – that's not foraging, that's called being a cheeky squirrel!

Identifying the Good Guys and the Bad Guys

Nature is full of amazing eats, but it also has some sneaky plants that are best left alone. Let's meet a few:

- **Good Guy:** Dandelion – These sunny flowers are not just pretty; they're pretty tasty, too! Every bit of the dandelion is edible, from the roots to the flowers.

- **Bad Guy:** Deadly Nightshade – Despite its cool name, this plant's dark berries are a no-go. They may look like something out of a fairy tale, but eating them is a villainous act against your belly.

Remember, there are many more plants out there, so keep your detective eyes open and your foraging guide handy!

Dangerous Areas to Avoid

While on our foraging quest, some areas are off-limits. These include:

- **Busy Roadsides:** Plants here can be covered in dust and pollution – yuck! Plus, it's not safe to be so close to traffic.

- **Mysterious Mushrooms:** Mushrooms are like the magicians of the plant world – some are safe, but others are super dangerous. Since they're tricky to tell apart, it's best to leave them be.

- **Industrial Areas:** Places that have factories or lots of machinery could have plants that have soaked up nasty chemicals. Not exactly the secret ingredient you want!

- **Unknown Territories:** If you're not familiar with an area, it's best to explore with an adult. Some places could have hidden dangers like swift rivers or sneaky cliffs.

Foraging Fun with Friends and Family

Foraging is way more fun when you do it with your favorite people. Plus, it's safer too!

- **Forage with a Buddy:** Always have a foraging friend or a grown-up with you. They can help you make safe choices and share in the fun.

- **Share Your Knowledge:** Teach your friends and family about safe foraging. Maybe you can even make a cool club with badges!

- **Enjoy Your Finds Together:** Having a meal with ingredients you've all foraged can be super exciting. Imagine saying, "I picked these berries!" at your next picnic.

Creative Corner: Make a Foraging Scrapbook!

As you learn about different plants, why not create a scrapbook? You can draw pictures, stick in photos, or even press leaves. It'll be your personal guide to the do's and don'ts of foraging, and it'll be as unique as your adventures.

To our brave foraging detectives, remember that nature is full of wonders, but we must treat it with respect and care. Use your smarts, stay safe, and keep those taste buds happy with only the best that the wild has to offer. You're not just a survivor; you're a nature hero!

And to the amazing adults who guide these young explorers, your wisdom is the compass that leads them to safe and joyful experiences. Keep encouraging their curiosity while ensuring their safety. Together, you'll create memories that are not just fun but also form the foundation of responsible wilderness exploration.

EDIBLE INSECTS: A TINY FEAST

In the world of wilderness survival, insects are not just creepy crawlies; they are a secret menu of nutrition. This might sound surprising, but in many cultures around the globe, insects are a regular part of the diet. For a young explorer, learning about edible insects is not just exciting, but it also opens a door to an unusual and often overlooked food source.

Before we leap into the world of edible insects, let's remember our survival superhero motto: "Safety first, adventure second!" Always check with an adult and make sure you're not allergic to any bugs before trying them. Now, let's spread our wings and fly into the buzz-worthy details!

1. The Buzz About Bugs

Insects are eaten by people all over the world, and they're packed with protein, vitamins, and minerals. Think of them as the tiny powerhouses of the wilderness. They can be found almost everywhere – under logs, in the grass, and even high up in the trees. But not all insects are safe to eat. Just like mushrooms in the forest, there are some rules we need to follow to avoid the ones that might make us feel yucky.

2. The Good Guys: Which Insects Can We Eat?

There are a bunch of insects that are safe and tasty to eat. Let's meet some of the superheroes of the edible insect world!

- **Grasshoppers and Crickets:** These hopping insects are like the popcorn of the bug world. They're crunchy and can be found in fields and meadows.

- **Ants:** Tiny but mighty, ants can be a tangy treat. Just be sure they're not the fiery kind that sting!

- **Mealworms:** These wiggly worms are actually beetle larvae, and they taste nutty when cooked.

- **Termites:** Found in wood, termites are like the peanut butter of the forest – smooth and rich in flavor.

3. The Bad Guys: Insects to Avoid

Now for the villains of the insect world. These are the bugs you should steer clear of:

- **Brightly Colored Insects:** If a bug is dressed in super bright colors, it's often nature's way of saying, "Stay away! I'm not for eating!"

- **Hairy or Spiky Insects:** Bugs with hair or spikes might be trying to protect themselves with stingers or poison, so it's best to leave them alone.

- **Disease Carriers:** Flies and mosquitoes can carry diseases, so they're not on the menu.

4. The How-To: Safely Catching and Preparing Insects

So, you've found an insect that's safe to eat. What's next? Follow these steps:

- **Catching:** Use a net or your hands to gently catch the insect. Be kind to our little friends, even if you're going to eat them.

- **Cleaning:** Wash the insects with clean water to get rid of any dirt or germs. It's like washing your fruits and veggies at home!

- **Cooking:** Always cook insects before eating them. This can mean roasting them over a fire or boiling them in water. Cooking makes sure that any tiny germs that might be on the bugs are zapped away!

5. The Yum Factor: Making Insects Tasty

Eating insects might sound a bit yuck at first, but with the right touch, they can be super yum! Here are some fun ways to make insects a delightful snack:

- **Seasoning:** Just like fries, insects can taste even better with a bit of seasoning. A sprinkle of salt or some herbs can go a long way.

- **Mixing:** Combine them with other foods. How about ants on a log (celery with peanut butter and raisins) with real ants instead of raisins for an extra crunch?

- **Creativity:** Get creative and come up with your own recipes. Maybe you'll invent the next big snack sensation!

6. The Brave Bites: Tasting Time

Now comes the moment of truth – tasting the insects. Take a small bite first to see how you like it. Remember, it's okay to be hesitant. It's a big step to try something so new and different!

7. The Sharing Circle: Respect for Nature

After our insect-tasting adventure, it's important to remember that we must respect nature. Insects are a part of the ecosystem, and we should only take what we need if we really need it. Think of it as borrowing from the wild pantry and always saying thank you.

8. The Safety Net: Allergies and Precautions

Just like with any new food, it's possible to be allergic to certain insects. If you ever feel weird after trying a bug, tell an adult immediately. It's always better to be safe than sorry when trying out survival snacks.

9. The Explorer's Journal: Document Your Discoveries

Keep an explorer's journal of the insects you've tasted and what you thought of them. It's like being a food critic for the wilderness!

10. The Adventure Continues: Keep Learning

There's so much more to discover about edible insects and survival. Keep learning, keep exploring, and always keep your curious spirit alive.

And there you have it, young survivalists! You've just taken a journey through the tiny, tasty world of edible insects. Remember, with great knowledge comes great responsibility. Use your new survival skills wisely and always with an adult's guidance. Until our next wild adventure, keep buzzing with excitement and curiosity!

COOKING IN THE WILD

Cooking in the wild is like unlocking a new level in an adventure game. It's about using your surroundings, a bit of creativity, and minimal tools to turn simple ingredients into a meal. This skill not only makes your outdoor experience more enjoyable but also teaches you about self-reliance and the value of simplicity.

Getting Started: Setting Up Your Kitchen

- **Find a Safe Spot**: Choose a flat area away from dry leaves or branches. If there's a breeze, make sure the wind is blowing away from your cooking area.

- **Create a Fire Pit**: If there isn't an existing fire ring, make a small circle with rocks. This will be your stove.

- **Gather Cooking Tools**: Use what you have. A pot or a pan, a spoon or stick for stirring, and a knife can be enough. In a pinch, even a clean, flat rock can serve as a cooking surface.

Fuel for Cooking

- **Use Small Sticks and Twigs**: These are easier to manage and create a more controlled heat.

- **Keep the Fire Small**: A huge fire isn't necessary. A small, steady flame is perfect for cooking.

Simple Cooking Methods

- **Boiling**: This is one of the easiest methods. Boil water for pasta, rice, or even wild plants you've foraged.

- **Grilling**: Place food directly on a grill or on a flat stone near the fire. Great for grilling fish or vegetables.

- **Roasting**: Use a stick to roast food over the flames. Think marshmallows or hot dogs, but also pieces of fruit or vegetables.

Safety While Cooking

- **Always Watch the Fire**: Never leave your cooking fire unattended.

- **Be Careful with Hot Tools**: Remember, the pot handle or the rock can get very hot.

- **Keep Water Nearby**: Have water ready in case you need to put out the fire quickly.

Cleaning Up

- **Dispose of Waste Properly**: Pack out all trash. Don't leave anything behind.

- **Clean Your Tools**: Use sand or a natural scrubber like a pinecone to clean your pots and pans.

Leaving No Trace

- **Put Out the Fire Completely**: Make sure the fire is entirely out before you leave. Scatter the cool ashes.

- **Restore the Area**: Leave the site as you found it, so others can enjoy the natural beauty too.

Respecting the Environment

- **Use Renewable Resources**: Gather fallen wood instead of cutting branches. Always forage sustainably.

- **Cook Responsibly**: Avoid using disposable plastic. Reusable containers and utensils are better for the environment.

- **Cooking as a Learning Experience** Outdoor cooking isn't just about the food; it's a learning experience. It's about adapting to your environment, being resourceful, and understanding the importance of conservation. Every meal cooked in the wild is a reminder of how much we rely on nature and how we must respect and protect it.

So, next time you're out in the wild, embrace the challenge of cooking with what you have. It's a chance to connect with nature, enjoy the simple pleasures of outdoor life, and create memories that will last a lifetime. Remember, the best ingredient in any outdoor cooking is a sense of adventure!

HUNTING ANIMALS FOR SURVIVAL

In the heart of the wilderness, where supermarkets and restaurants are miles away, understanding the basics of hunting and trapping can be an invaluable skill. It's about more than just catching food; it's about connecting with nature, learning patience, and respecting the circle of life.

Have you ever wondered what it would be like to be out in the wild, surrounded by the rustling trees, the chirping birds, and the whispers of the wind? Imagine you're on an adventure, maybe hiking through a thick forest or camping under the stars. Suddenly, you realize you're going to need food to keep your energy up for all the amazing activities you've planned. But oh no, you've run out of snacks! What do you do?

This is where the ancient skill of hunting and trapping comes in handy. Now, before you think of hunting as just chasing animals, it's important to know that it's much more than that. It's about being in tune with nature, understanding the balance of the ecosystem, and learning how to responsibly and respectfully find food if you ever really need to. It's a survival skill that goes way back to the time of early explorers and adventurers – just like you!

Why Learn to Hunt and Trap?

First off, remember, hunting and trapping are skills that are only used in a survival situation. It's not about being harmful to animals or the environment; it's about being resourceful and respectful. It's like having a secret tool in your adventure kit that you only use when you truly need it.

In the wild, animals are part of a food web, a loop of who-eats-who. Sometimes, humans are part of that web too, especially in survival situations. Knowing how to hunt and trap means you can find food to keep your body strong and your mind sharp. Plus, you get to learn all about animal behaviors, tracks, and habitats, turning you into a real-life wildlife detective!

Safety First!

Before we dive into the nitty-gritty of hunting and trapping, we must talk about safety. Just like any other outdoor activity, you should never go on a hunting adventure without an adult who's trained in these skills. Also, you need to understand the laws and regulations about hunting in your area because it's important to follow rules that help protect you and the animals.

Always handle any hunting tools with care and respect. Remember, these aren't toys; they're tools that serve a purpose. And most importantly, you should always be aware of your surroundings to make sure you, and everyone with you, is safe.

The Basics of Hunting and Trapping

Hunting and trapping are two different things. Hunting usually involves going out and looking for animals to harvest, while trapping involves setting up a device to catch an animal for you.

When hunters go out, they have to be very quiet, very patient, and super observant. They look for signs like animal tracks, nibbled plants, or even animal homes. Trappers set up traps in places where animals are likely to pass by. Both hunting and trapping require a lot of knowledge about the animal you're trying to find.

Tools of the Trade

In history, people used all sorts of tools for hunting – like bows and arrows, slingshots, and spears. For trapping, they crafted snares and pits. Nowadays, we have modern tools, but in a survival situation, you might need to use what nature provides. That could mean making a simple snare out of a vine or a fishing hook out of a twig!

Hunting and Trapping with Respect

This is super important, friends. Hunting and trapping should always be done with a deep respect for nature and the animals. You should only take what you need, and nothing more. It's about balance and understanding that every animal has a role in the environment.

Becoming a Responsible Hunter

To be a responsible hunter, start by learning all you can about wildlife. Read books, watch documentaries, and maybe even join a nature club. The more you know, the better you'll understand when and how to use these skills. And always, always follow the rules and guidelines set by experts.

Fun Facts and Tips

Did you know that different animals leave different kinds of tracks? By learning to identify these tracks, you can tell which animals have been in the area. And here's a cool tip: animals often follow natural paths like riverbanks or the edges of forests, so these can be good places to look for signs of wildlife.

The Big Picture

While hunting and trapping for survival are important skills, it's equally important to learn about conservation. That means using natural resources wisely so they'll be around for a long, long time. It's all about taking care of our planet and the amazing creatures we share it with.

So, there you have it, brave adventurers. Hunting and trapping are ancient survival skills that require knowledge, patience, and respect. Remember, these skills are a last resort for survival and should be used wisely and responsibly. Keep exploring, stay curious, and respect the great outdoors, and you'll be on your way to becoming a true survival expert!

CHAPTER 6

FINDING YOUR WAY

Navigating the great outdoors is an adventure in itself. It's like a puzzle where the sky, the land, and even the stars join hands to guide you. This chapter is all about finding your way, whether you're on a well-marked trail or deep in the wilderness. It's about understanding the art and science of navigation, which not only keeps you safe but also turns you into a savvy explorer.

Getting lost can happen to anyone but knowing what to do if it happens is a skill that's as important as any survival technique. It's about staying calm, using your head, and remembering some key tips and tricks.

But what if you don't have a map or a compass? No problem! The world around you is filled with natural signposts. From the position of the sun to the pattern of the stars, nature offers clues for those who know how to read them. You'll learn how to use these ancient techniques to find your way, just like explorers did long ago.

Understanding the landscape is another crucial skill. The shape of the land, the flow of a river, and even the types of plants can tell you where you are and which way to go. Landmarks and terrain features become your guideposts, helping you navigate through nature's vastness.

While traditional navigation skills are essential, modern technology has given us tools like GPS, which can be a huge help. We'll explore how to use these tools wisely without over-relying on them. Because sometimes, batteries die, signals get lost, but the skills you've learned and the knowledge you carry are always with you.

So, get ready to embark on a journey of discovery, where the path isn't just about getting from point A to point B, but about understanding the language of the earth and sky. This chapter isn't just about finding your way in the wilderness; it's about finding a deeper connection with the world around you.

WHAT TO DO IF YOU ARE LOST?

Imagine this: You're on a field trip in the forest, and you stray a bit from the group to check out a really cool bug. When you look up, you realize you can't see your friends anymore. Yikes! You feel your heart start to race. What do you do?

Stay Calm and Don't Panic - First things first, take a deep breath. Inhale... exhale. Remember, staying calm is your superpower when you're lost. Panicking is like adding fog to a cloudy day—it makes everything more confusing. Your brain works best when it's calm, so if you feel worried, take a few more deep breaths.

Stay Put - Now that you're a calm captain, it's important to stay where you are. Think of yourself as a tree rooted in place. This makes it easier for rescuers to find you. If you move around, you might get even further from your group, and we don't want that.

Get Noticed - It's time to turn yourself into a human lighthouse! Make yourself visible. If you have a bright jacket or a piece of clothing, put it on or tie it to a stick to wave in the air. If it's safe, find an open area, like a clearing, so you can be seen from a distance.

Use Your Whistle - Do you have a whistle? Three sharp blasts on a whistle is a universal signal for "Help!" It's like sending out an SOS text message, but with sound. Keep blowing that whistle at intervals, and someone will come to find you.

Make a Survival Bracelet - Guess what? You can make a cool survival bracelet before you even head out on your adventure. It can hold some handy gear like a whistle, a little compass, or even some string. You'll learn how to make one in Chapter 8.4, so don't forget to check it out!

Create a Shelter - If it seems like you might be out for a while, it's time to get crafty. Find some branches or a big fallen tree and make a little shelter. This isn't just any fort; it's your personal shield against the wind and rain. Plus, it gives you a home base.

Signal with a Mirror - If you have a small mirror or any shiny object, you can use it to signal for help. Reflect the sun's rays toward where you think people might be. It's like using a flashlight in the daytime, and it can catch a rescaper's eye from far away.

Stay Warm and Dry - Keep as warm and dry as you can. If it's cold, huddle into your shelter and wrap yourself up like a burrito in any extra clothes you have. If it's sunny, find some shade so you don't get too hot. Your body is like a car—it runs best when it's not too cold or too hot.

Find Water - If you're going to be lost for more than a day, you'll need water. But remember, only drink from a stream or river if you have a grown-up who can check if it's safe or if you have a water purification method. We'll talk all about finding and purifying water in Chapter 9.3.

Leave Clues - You can be a detective in reverse! Leave clues for rescuers to find you. Break branches, make arrow shapes with rocks, or create a trail with something colorful. These clues are like breadcrumbs leading right to you.

Use the "Hug-A-Tree" Method - If remembering all this is too much, just think "Hug-A-Tree." It's easy: stay calm, stay put, and hug a tree. It's a good way to remember not to wander off, and it keeps you safe while someone comes to find you.

Remember, You Are Not Alone - Even when you're lost, you're not alone. Think about all the people who care about you and are looking for you. They've got your back!

Talk to the Trees - This might sound silly, but if you're feeling lonely or scared, talk to the trees or sing a song. It keeps your spirits up and, who knows, maybe the birds will sing along!

Practice Makes Perfect - With your parents or guardians, practice these steps in a safe place. It's like having a fire drill at home—you hope you never need it, but it's good to know what to do just in case.

And there you have it, brave adventurers—your guide to staying calm and safe if you ever find yourself lost. Remember, everyone who explores the great outdoors can sometimes take a wrong turn, but with these tips, you'll be prepared to handle it like a pro.

Navigating without a map or compass is like solving a riddle. It makes you more aware of your environment and connects you deeply with nature. These skills are not just about finding your way; they're about understanding the natural world and feeling at home in it. So next time you're outdoors, look around, and see what nature is trying to tell you. With practice, you'll become a natural navigator, confidently finding your way by reading the language of the land and sky.

USING THE SKY (STARS, SUN, AND MOON AS NAVIGATION AIDS)

Have you ever looked up at the night sky and wondered if those twinkling stars could help you find your way? Or watched the sun set and thought about which direction it was going? In this fascinating world of outdoor adventures, the sky is not just a beautiful backdrop; it's a map and a compass all rolled into one. Let's unravel the secrets of using the sky - the stars, sun, and moon - as navigation aids.

Navigating with the Stars For centuries, travelers and explorers have used the stars to navigate. The key is finding the North Star, known as Polaris. It almost always points true north. You can find Polaris by locating the Big Dipper, a prominent group of seven stars. The two stars at the end of the 'bowl' of the Big Dipper point straight to Polaris.

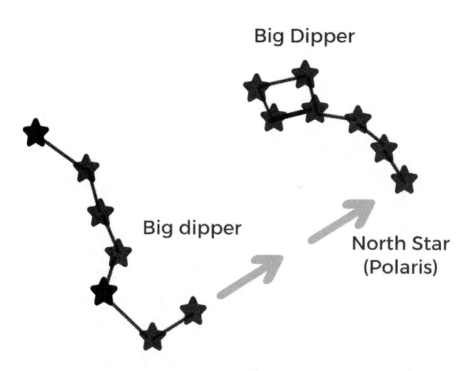

In the Southern Hemisphere, you won't see the North Star. Instead, you can use the Southern Cross constellation to find south. First, locate the bright stars that form a cross. Then, draw an imaginary line from the top of the Cross to the bottom (towards the horizon) and extend it five times its length. The point where this line ends points south.

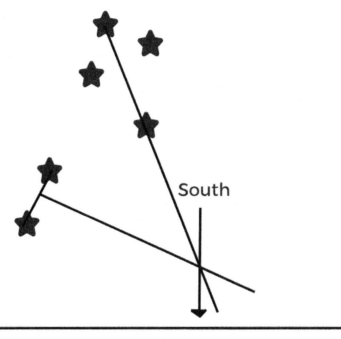

Sun for Direction: The sun rises in the east and sets in the west - a simple yet powerful guide for direction. In the morning, the sun is in the eastern part of the sky. By noon, it's almost directly overhead and then moves toward the west. If you stand with your right shoulder towards the sun in the morning, you will be facing north. In the evening, do the opposite: stand with your left shoulder towards the setting sun to face north.

Moon Phases and Direction: The moon can also be a subtle guide. If you see a crescent moon, draw an imaginary line connecting the two points of the crescent and extend it down to the horizon. In the Northern Hemisphere, this point indicates approximately south. In the Southern Hemisphere, it indicates approximately north.

Understanding the Movement of the Sky: The sky changes throughout the night and year. The stars rotate around Polaris in the Northern Hemisphere, making it seem like they are moving in a circle. Knowing some key constellations and their movements can help you estimate time and direction during the night.

Using Shadows and Sticks: During the day, you can use a stick and its shadow to find direction. Place a stick upright in the ground and mark where the shadow falls. Wait about 15 minutes and mark the end of the shadow again. Draw a line between the two points. In the Northern Hemisphere, the first point is west and the second is east.

The sky is a timeless map that has guided humans for millennia. Learning to read it is not just a survival skill, but also a way to connect with our ancestors and the natural world. It's a reminder that sometimes, the simplest tools are the most powerful. So, next time you're outside, whether during the day or at night, take a moment to look up and read the sky. It's a storybook, a map, and a compass, all waiting to be discovered.

LANDMARKS AND TERRAIN FEATURES (HOW TO USE NATURAL MARKERS FOR DIRECTION)

The natural world is full of signs and markers that can guide us on our journeys. Just like sailors once used stars to navigate the seas, you can use landmarks and terrain features to find your way through forests, mountains, or any outdoor landscape. This skill is about observing and interpreting the natural world around you, turning every outdoor adventure into a fascinating experience of discovery and learning.

Understanding Landmarks: A landmark is any natural or man-made feature that is easily recognizable and can help you determine your location or direction. This could be a distinctive tree, a uniquely shaped rock, a mountain peak, or even a man-made structure like a bridge or tower. The key is to choose landmarks that stand out and are unlikely to change over time.

Making a Mental Map: When you start your journey, take a moment to observe your surroundings. Identify a few landmarks and remember their locations. As you move, keep track of these landmarks in relation to your movement. This helps you form a mental map of the area, assisting you in understanding where you are at any given time.

Using Terrain Features: Terrain features like hills, valleys, rivers, and streams can also help you navigate. For instance, rivers often flow from higher elevations to lower ones and can lead you to larger bodies of water or settlements. Hills and mountain ranges tend to run in specific directions, which can be used to determine your general heading.

The Shape of the Land: Observe the shape of the land, known as topography. A topographical map can help you understand the terrain before you start, but you can also read the land as you go. Notice how the land rises and falls, where it slopes, and where it flattens out. These patterns can give you clues about where you are and where you're headed.

Sun and Shadow: The position of the sun in the sky can help you understand direction. In the Northern Hemisphere, the sun is in the southern part of the sky for most of the day, casting shadows to the north. This can help you determine east and west.

Water Flow: In many landscapes, water flows in a consistent direction, often towards a larger river, lake, or the ocean. By observing the direction of a stream or river, you can get a sense of general direction. However, be aware that waterways can meander and aren't always a straight path to civilization.

Create Landmarks: If you're in an area where natural landmarks are scarce, create your own. Stacking rocks, tying a piece of fabric to a tree, or making a small pile of sticks can help you mark your path and find your way back if needed.

Remembering Your Path: As you move, frequently look back to see how the landscape appears from the opposite direction. This can be invaluable when you need to return the way you came.

Staying Oriented: Keep checking your landmarks and terrain features as you travel. This helps you stay oriented and prevents you from walking in circles, a common issue when lost.

Navigating using landmarks and terrain features is an engaging way to interact with nature. It sharpens your observation skills, deepens your connection with the environment, and enhances your understanding of the natural world. With practice, you'll develop an intuitive sense of direction, making you a confident and competent navigator, ready for any adventure that awaits.

STAYING ON TRACK (THE IMPORTANCE OF STICKING TO TRAILS AND PATHS)

When you're venturing into the great outdoors, whether it's a lush forest, a mountain range, or a sprawling national park, trails and paths are more than just lines on the ground. They are carefully created guides that ensure safety, protect nature, and offer an enjoyable experience. Staying on these designated trails is crucial, not just for your well-being but for preserving the beauty and balance of the natural environment around you.

Safety First: Trails are designed to be navigated safely. They avoid hazardous areas that might not be immediately visible, like unstable ground, steep drops, or dense areas that could be home to wildlife. Wandering off the trail can lead you into risky situations. Trails also ensure that you are within areas that search and rescue teams can reach in case of an emergency.

Protecting the Environment: The wilderness is a delicate ecosystem, and trails are designed to minimize human impact on these environments. Straying off the path can lead to trampling plants, disturbing wildlife, and causing erosion. By sticking to the trail, you're helping to protect the natural habitats and ensuring that they remain pristine for future adventurers.

Respecting Wildlife: Wild animals are more likely to be disturbed by humans wandering off the path. Trails allow you to observe wildlife without invading their space. Remember, for us it's an adventure, but for them, it's home. Staying on the path helps maintain a respectful distance between you and the wildlife.

Finding Your Way: Trails are marked for a reason. They guide you to significant points, offer the best views, and ensure you can find your way back. By staying on these paths, you reduce the risk of getting lost. Many trails have signs and markers to provide direction and information, making your journey informative and enjoyable.

Maintaining the Beauty for Others: Imagine if every visitor decided to create their own path. The wilderness would quickly become a web of crisscrossing lines, damaging its natural beauty. By staying on the trail, you help preserve the wilderness not just for the environment but also for other people who will follow in your footsteps.

Enhancing Your Experience: Trails are often designed to showcase the best of the natural world. They take you to the most beautiful spots, offer the best views, and provide a path through the most interesting environments. By following these trails, you're guaranteed a richer and more fulfilling outdoor experience.

Learning to Read Trails: Understanding trail markers, signs, and maps is an important skill. They use symbols and colors to convey information about the trail's difficulty, direction, and points of interest. Learning to read these signs enhances your ability to navigate and enjoy your surroundings.

Being a Responsible Adventurer: Staying on the trail is a sign of a responsible and respectful adventurer. It shows that you care about the safety of yourself and others, the protection of the environment, and the preservation of the wilderness for future generations.

Trails and paths are there to guide you, protect you, and show you the wonders of the natural world. They are the result of careful planning and consideration for the environment and visitors. Sticking to these paths is a mark of a conscientious and responsible explorer. So, when you're out on your next adventure, remember the importance of staying on track. It ensures a safe, enjoyable, and sustainable experience for everyone.

MODERN TECHNOLOGY IN NAVIGATION (INCORPORATING GPS AND OTHER TOOLS)

In today's world, technology has woven itself into almost every aspect of our lives, and outdoor navigation is no exception. The emergence of GPS (Global Positioning System) and various other technological tools has revolutionized the way we explore the great outdoors. These modern marvels have made navigation more accessible, accurate, and safe, providing adventurers with invaluable assistance on their journeys.

GPS: Your Digital Compass: The most significant advancement in navigation technology is the GPS device. GPS receivers use satellites to pinpoint your exact location on Earth. These handy gadgets can tell you where you are, which direction you're facing, how high you are, and even how fast you're moving. They come in various forms, from dedicated GPS units to apps on smartphones.

Smartphone Apps: Navigation at Your Fingertips: Smartphones have become powerful navigation tools, thanks to a plethora of apps. These apps offer features like detailed maps, trail guides, and even the ability to track your route. Some apps work offline, which is crucial when exploring areas with no cell service. However, it's important to keep in mind that smartphones have limitations, like battery life and the potential for damage in rugged conditions.

Using Technology Wisely: While these tools are incredibly useful, relying solely on technology can be risky. Batteries die, signals get lost, and devices can fail. It's essential to use technology as a supplement to traditional navigation skills, not a replacement. Always carry a paper map and compass as backups and know how to use them.

Geocaching: The High-Tech Treasure Hunt: An exciting aspect of modern navigation is geocaching, a worldwide treasure hunt game. Participants use GPS devices to hide and seek containers called "geocaches" at specific locations marked by coordinates. It's a fun way to practice navigation skills and explore new places.

Emergency Beacons and Trackers: For those venturing into remote or high-risk areas, emergency beacons and trackers can be lifesavers. These devices can send distress signals and your location to rescue services, providing peace of mind for both adventurers and their loved ones.

Drones: A Bird's Eye View: Drones have also found a place in outdoor exploration. They offer a unique perspective, capturing aerial views of landscapes and potentially scouting areas that are difficult to assess from the ground. However, it's important to use drones responsibly and adhere to regulations, especially in protected natural areas.

The Importance of Digital Etiquette: While using technology, it's important to practice digital etiquette. Be mindful of others who may be seeking a tech-free experience in nature. Also, respect privacy and avoid capturing images of people without their consent.

Educational Tools for Young Explorers: For children, technology can make learning about navigation and the natural world more engaging. Apps that teach map reading, star identification, and trail tracking can be excellent educational tools, sparking curiosity and a love for exploration.

Incorporating modern technology into navigation brings a new dimension to outdoor adventures. It enhances our abilities to explore, discover, and connect with the world around us. However, balancing the use of these tools with traditional skills and an appreciation for the natural environment is key.

CHAPTER 7

WILDERNESS FIRST AID

Ever been on a hike or a camping trip and got a scratch or a bruise? Ouch, right? Well, that's where Wilderness First Aid comes in. It's all about knowing what to do when someone gets hurt while you're out exploring nature. This isn't just for adults; kids like you can be super helpers too!

Imagine you're hiking through a forest with your best friends, following a map to find the hidden treasure. Suddenly, one of your friends' trips over a root and scrapes their knee. Oh no! But don't worry, you're prepared because you've learned wilderness first aid. You whip out your colorful first aid kit, and with a few simple steps, your friend is smiling again, ready to continue the quest. How cool is that?

The Superhero First Aid Kit

First things first, every wilderness detective needs their superhero toolkit. So, what's in this magical box? Let's open it and see:

- **Bandages and Plasters**: Like little knights protecting a castle, these stick onto cuts and scrapes to guard against germs.

- **Antiseptic Wipes**: These are like mini mops, cleaning up any dirt from a wound so it can heal super-fast.

- **Tweezers**: Imagine these as your tiny rescue tongs, perfect for removing splinters from your skin.

- **Gloves**: Superheroes wear capes, but wilderness first-aid heroes wear gloves to keep their hands clean while they help.

- **Scissors**: Not for arts and crafts this time! These are for cutting bandages or clothing if needed.

- **A Cold Pack**: Think of it as a chill charm, soothing any swelling or bruises.

Remember, the most important thing in your first aid kit is knowledge – knowing what to do with all these cool tools!

The ABCs of First Aid

When someone is hurt, there's an easy way to remember what to do. It's as simple as ABC!

- **A** is for Airway: Make sure nothing is blocking the person's breathing.

- **B** is for Breathing: Check if they're breathing okay.

- **C** is for Circulation: Look for any bleeding and get ready to act like a hero if you need to stop it.

Cuts and Scrapes – The Mini Battle Scars

If your friend gets a cut, don't just stand there like a statue! Here's what you can do:

1. Wash your hands or put on those superhero gloves.

2. Use an antiseptic wipe to clean around the cut – be gentle, don't make your friend jump like a kangaroo!

3. Dry the area with a clean cloth or gauze and then put on a bandage or plaster.

Twists and Shouts – Dealing with Sprains

Sometimes, ankles twist in ways they shouldn't, and it can hurt a lot! If this happens:

1. Help your friend sit down, and don't let them use their detective skills to solve the mystery of walking on a sprain.

2. Put something cold on the sprain – this is where your chill charm comes in handy. It helps to make the boo-boo feel better.

3. Keep the sprain up high, like it's on top of a mountain. This helps keep the swelling down.

Be a Wilderness Whisperer – Dealing with Animal Bites

Animals in the wild are usually more scared of you than you are of them. But sometimes, they might get surprised and bite. Here's what to do if that happens:

1. Stay calm – remember, you're a cool wilderness detective.

2. Wash the bite with soap and water, and then use those antiseptic wipes from your kit.

3. Cover the bite with a clean bandage and keep an eye on it. If it gets red, swells up, or your friend feels sick, tell an adult right away.

Poison Patrol – Plants and Bugs

Some plants and bugs can be meanies, leaving itchy rashes or stings. If you touch a plant like poison ivy or get stung by a bee, don't panic!

1. For plants, rinse the area with water and don't scratch – even if it feels like you have ants in your pants!

2. For bug stings, if there's a stinger, use your tweezers to gently pull it out.

3. Apply a cold pack to say "chill out" to any swelling.

Practice Makes Perfect

The best way to become a first aid superhero is to practice. With your parents or caregivers, you can have fun role-playing different scenarios. Pretend one of you is injured and the other is the first aid hero! This way, if something really happens, you'll know exactly what to do.

Wilderness First Aid Badge of Honor

Once you've learned all these first aid skills, you'll earn your Wilderness First Aid Badge of Honor. Wear it proudly on your adventure gear! It shows you're ready to take on the wild, care for your fellow explorers, and make sure the only thing you bring back from your adventures are awesome memories and maybe a little mud on your boots.

CUTS AND SCRAPES: TREATING MINOR WOUNDS AND PREVENTING INFECTION

When you're out adventuring in the great outdoors, a scrape or a cut might pop up. It's all part of the adventure! But no worries, treating these little surprises is easier than you think. Here's how to do it step by step, so you can get back to having fun in no time!

Step 1: Stay Calm and Check the Wound The first thing to do is take a deep breath. If you or a friend gets a cut, it's important to stay calm. Then, gently check how big or deep the cut is. Small scratches are usually no big deal, but if it's bigger or bleeding a lot, finding an adult is the best first step.

Step 2: Clean It Up If it's just a small scrape, your next move is to clean it. Rinse it gently with clean water. This helps wash away dirt or tiny rocks. No need for soap – water does the trick! If there's no water around, use a clean wet cloth or a wipe from your first aid kit.

Step 3: Dry and Protect After cleaning, pat the area dry with a clean cloth or a piece of gauze. Be gentle – no rubbing! Then, it's time to protect the cut. Grab a bandage from your first aid kit and cover it up. Bandages keep out dirt and germs, which helps your cut heal without getting infected.

Step 4: Keep an Eye on It Now that the cut is all cleaned and covered, keep an eye on it. If it starts looking red, swollen, or if there's pus, tell an adult. These can be signs of infection. It's rare, but it's good to be careful. If the bandage gets wet or dirty, replace it with a new one.

Step 5: Healing Time Your body is amazing at healing. Small cuts usually get better in a few days. While it's healing, try not to pick at the scab. It might be tempting, but the scab is your body's natural bandage, keeping the cut clean and protected while it heals.

Step 6: When to Seek More Help Sometimes, a cut might need a bit more care, especially if it's deep or won't stop bleeding. If that happens, it's important to get help from an adult or a doctor. They can make sure everything is okay and give extra care if needed.

Step 7: Prevention is Key Preventing cuts and scrapes is part of the adventure too! Wearing the right clothes like long pants and sleeves can help protect your skin. Being aware of where you're walking or climbing is also important. And always have your first aid kit handy – it's your adventure buddy!

Step 8: Learning and Sharing Now that you know how to handle cuts and scrapes, you can share this knowledge with your friends and family. Teaching others what you've learned is not just cool, it's super helpful. You become a part of keeping everyone safe and happy on outdoor adventures.

Remember:

- Small cuts and scrapes are common and easy to handle.
- Cleaning the wound is the most important step to prevent infection.
- A bandage is like a shield, protecting the cut as it heals.
- Your body is great at healing; give it time and care.
- If in doubt, always ask for help from an adult or a doctor.

So, there you have it, the simple steps to take care of cuts and scrapes. It's a basic but super important skill for any young explorer. By knowing what to do, you not only take care of yourself but also become someone others can rely on. That's a big part of being an adventurer – being prepared, staying safe, and helping out. Keep exploring and keep safe!

TREATING COMMON INJURIES: PRACTICAL TREATMENT TECHNIQUES

Outdoors, sometimes a few bumps and bruises happen. It's part of the adventure! But knowing what to do when common injuries occur is super important. Imagine you're in the middle of a thrilling quest through the Enchanted Forest of Evergreen. Suddenly, ouch! You've stumbled and scraped your knee. Don't worry, my brave friend; with these practical treatment techniques, you'll be back on your quest in no time!

Treating Bruises: Bruises are like little reminders of your adventures. They happen when you bump into something, and your skin turns a bit blue or purple. Here's what to do:

1.   Rest the bruised area. If it's on your leg or arm, try not to use it too much.

2.   Put a cold pack or a bag of frozen peas wrapped in a cloth on the bruise. This helps reduce swelling and the color.

3.   Keep the bruised area raised if possible. This means if it's your leg or arm, try to keep it up on a pillow.

Handling Sprains: Sprains occur when you twist or turn your ankle or wrist more than it likes. Here's the way to take care of them:

1.   Rest is key. Don't try to walk or use the sprained part too much.

2.   Ice helps a lot. Use a cold pack or ice wrapped in a towel for about 20 minutes.

3.   Wrap the sprained area with a bandage, but not too tight! It should feel snug, not uncomfortable.

4.   Elevate it. If it's an ankle or wrist, prop it up on pillows.

Caring for Small Burns: Sometimes small burns can happen, maybe from a campfire spark. Don't worry, you can handle this too!

1. Run cool (not cold) water over the burn area for a few minutes. This helps soothe the skin.

2. Dry it gently with a clean cloth.

3. Cover the burn with a sterile, non-sticky bandage. This protects it while it heals.

Treating Insect Bites and Stings: Insects are part of nature, but their bites or stings can be annoying. Here's what to do:

1. For bites, wash the area with soap and water.

2. Apply a cold pack to reduce swelling and itchiness.

3. If it's a sting and the stinger is still in the skin, gently scrape it out sideways with something like a credit card. Avoid using tweezers, as it can squeeze more venom into the skin.

When to Get Help: Sometimes, an injury might need more care than you can give. If someone is in a lot of pain, if a burn is bigger than a small scrape, or if a sprain or cut seems very bad, get an adult or a doctor to help.

Preventing Injuries: You can also do a lot to prevent these injuries:

- Wear protective gear like helmets, knee pads, and gloves when you're biking or skating.

- Be careful around fires and hot surfaces.

- Watch where you're going to avoid sprains and bruises.

- Use insect repellent to keep bugs away.

Being prepared for these common injuries means you can keep having fun without too much worry. Always have a first aid kit with you, and know where to find an adult if you need help. Remember, treating injuries is just another part of being a great adventurer. Stay safe, and keep exploring!

INFECTION WATCH: IDENTIFYING AND RESPONDING TO SIGNS OF INFECTION

Infections are like unwanted guests on your outdoor adventures. They can sneak in through cuts or scrapes but knowing how to spot and handle them is a big part of staying safe. Let's dive into the signs of infection and what to do about them.

Spotting an Infection:

Infections are like tiny invaders trying to crash your body's party. They're caused by germs such as bacteria, viruses, and fungi. When you get a cut or a scrape, these germs see an open door and think, "Party time!" But don't worry, you've got your own team of defenders—your immune system. It's like your body's own superhero squad, ready to fight off these pesky party crashers.

Redness and Swelling: If a cut or scrape gets red and puffy, that's a common sign. The area around the wound might look a bit more red than usual.

Warmth: An infected area often feels warm. If you touch it gently, it might feel hotter than the skin around it.

Pain: Infections can be painful. If a wound starts hurting more than when you first got it, that's a signal.

Pus: This is a yellowish or greenish liquid that might come out of the wound. It's a clear sign the body is fighting germs.

Fever: Sometimes, if an infection is more serious, it might cause a fever. This means your body's temperature goes up as it fights the infection.

What to Do if You Spot an Infection:

- **Clean Again:** If the wound looks a bit infected, clean it gently once more with water.

- **Use Antiseptic:** Applying an antiseptic cream or solution, which you can find in your first aid kit, helps fight off the germs.

- **New Bandage:** After cleaning and applying antiseptic, put on a fresh bandage to keep it clean.

- **Tell an Adult:** It's important to let an adult know. They can help decide if you need to see a doctor.

- **Rest:** Giving your body time to heal is important. Try to take it easy and not stress the wounded area.

- **Going to a Doctor:** If the signs of infection don't go away or if you have a fever, it's time to see a doctor. Doctors have more tools to treat infections, like antibiotics, which are like special fighters against germs.

- **Preventing Infections:** Preventing infections is better than treating them:

- **Keep Wounds Clean:** Always clean a cut or scrape right away.

- **Use Bandages:** Covering a wound with a bandage keeps germs out.

- **Don't Touch:** Avoid touching the wound too much with your hands.

- **Change Bandages:** If a bandage gets dirty or wet, change it with a new, clean one.

- **Hand Washing:** Washing your hands regularly is a good habit, especially before and after treating a wound.

- **Staying Alert and Ready:** Being able to notice signs of infection means you're becoming a smart and responsible adventurer. Keeping your first aid kit stocked, knowing how to use it, and understanding when to get help are key skills. Remember, every explorer needs to be ready for a little bump in the road and knowing about infections is part of that journey.

- **Your Role in Safety:** By understanding infections, you're not just taking care of yourself, but you're also helping to keep your friends and family safe. Share what you know about spotting and treating infections. Together, you can all enjoy your outdoor adventures, knowing you're prepared to handle any small mishaps that come your way.

Infections might sound scary, but with this knowledge, you're well-equipped to handle them. Keeping an eye out for these signs and knowing what to do makes you an even more awesome and responsible adventurer. Stay curious, stay safe, and keep exploring the wonders of the outdoors!

WHY A FIRST AID KIT IS A MUST!
(WHAT TO PACK FOR EMERGENCY CARE)

Have you ever imagined yourself as a hero in an adventure story, where you're the one who saves the day with your quick thinking and a trusty first aid kit? Well, guess what? You don't have to be just in a story to be that hero! Whether you're out hiking in the great wilderness, camping under the stars, or just playing in your backyard, a first aid kit is your secret superpower for safety.

So, why is a first aid kit a must-have gadget in your adventure gear? Let's dive into the magical world of first aid and discover how this small box can make a big difference!

The Magic Box of Care

A first aid kit is like a treasure chest filled with special tools that can help fix up scrapes, soothe stings, and take care of those "oops" moments faster than you can say "Abracadabra!" It's your first line of defense when someone gets hurt, and it helps make sure that small injuries don't turn into big problems.

What to Pack in Your Superhero Kit

Imagine your first aid kit is like Batman's utility belt—it has everything you need for emergency care! Here's a list of items to include in your kit, but remember, the most important thing you can pack is your knowledge of how to use them.

1. **Adhesive Bandages (Aka Plasters):** These are like little hugs for your cuts and scrapes. They come in all sizes for small to larger owies.

2. **Sterile Gauze Pads:** These are like pillows for larger boo-boos. They help cover and protect wounds from dirt and germs.

3. **Adhesive Tape:** Think of it as the glue that holds the gauze pads in place. It's super sticky, so it keeps the pads from falling off.

4. **Antiseptic Wipes:** These are like little warriors that fight off the bad germs that try to sneak into cuts and scrapes.

5. **Tweezers:** These are like mini tongs that can remove splinters from your skin. They are the knights in shining armor for your fingers and toes!

6. **Scissors:** These aren't for arts and crafts! They're for cutting tape or clothing if you need to get to a wound quickly.

7. **Disposable Gloves:** These keep your hands clean when you're helping someone else, like a superhero's gloves that protect their secret identity.

8. **Antibiotic Ointment:** This is like a healing potion for your cuts. It helps keep them clean and makes them feel better faster.

9. **Cold Pack:** This is like a mini snowman that can help reduce swelling from bumps and bruises. No freezer required!

10. **Thermometer:** This tool checks if someone has a fever, letting you know if their body is fighting a dragon (or, you know, an infection).

11. **Emergency Contact Information:** This is like a map that tells you who to call or where to go if the adventure gets too wild.

12. **First Aid Manual:** This book is your guide to using all the tools in your kit. It's like having a wise wizard by your side.

How to Be a First Aid Wizard

Now that you know what goes into your kit, it's time to learn the spells—oops, I mean the skills! You'll need to know how to clean a cut, what to do if someone is choking, and how to use everything in your first aid kit. Always ask an adult to help you practice these skills.

The Responsibility of Power

With great power comes great responsibility, young adventurers. When you carry a first aid kit, you're promising to be careful and only use it when it's really needed. It's not a toy, but a powerful tool for helping yourself and others.

Adventure Safely and Smartly

Remember, the best way to be safe is to avoid getting hurt in the first place. Be smart and careful when you're exploring. But if an accident does happen, you'll be ready with your handy-dandy first aid kit!

Sharing the Knowledge

Make sure your friends and family know about your first aid kit, too. You can teach them what you've learned, and maybe even practice together. It's like forming your own team of safety superheroes!

First Aid Fun

Finally, let's make learning about first aid fun! You can create your own first aid kit with your favorite stickers, or even make a game out of learning first aid steps. Who can remember what to do for a bee sting? What about a sunburn? The more you practice, the better prepared you'll be.

So, young heroes, are you ready to embrace the power of the first aid kit? By packing your kit with care and learning to use it with wisdom, you'll be the guardian of your adventures, the healer of harms, and the champion of playtime safety. Go forth and explore, but always be prepared!

Remember, the outdoors is full of surprises, and a first aid kit ensures you're prepared for them. It's a small step in your preparation that makes a huge difference. Every time you pack your kit, you're taking responsibility for your safety and the safety of those around you. That's what being a true explorer is all about!

CHAPTER 8

WILDERNESS COMMUNICATION

Have you ever wondered how to get help if you're lost in the woods or how to tell your family you're okay during an adventure? Let's find out how to use some neat tools and tricks to talk to people, even when you're far away!

First, let's talk about whistles, mirrors, and flags. These are your best friends in the wilderness. If you blow a whistle loudly, someone far away can hear it. Three short blasts mean you need help. Mirrors are not just for looking at yourself. If you catch the sun's light and flash it towards someone, they can see it from far away. And flags? They're great for signaling too. You can make a flag from anything bright and wave it to catch attention.

Next, there's the SOS signal. It's a universal way of saying, "Help me!" You can make an SOS signal in many ways. You can draw it in the sand, make it with stones, or even use lights at night. Just remember, it's three short signals, three long ones, and then three short ones again.

Now, let's chat about Morse code. It's like a secret language using dots and dashes. With Morse code, you can tap out a message. For example, a simple "SOS" in Morse code is "... --- ...". It's fun to learn and can be really useful.

We also have cool tech stuff like satellite phones, radios, and GPS devices. These gadgets are helpful for staying in touch or finding your way. But remember, always have a backup plan because sometimes these gadgets might not work.

Lastly, it's super important to know emergency phone numbers. These numbers are different in different places. It's like having a direct line to superheroes who can come to save the day. Always keep these numbers with you, just in case.

Before heading out on your adventure, make sure to tell someone about your plans. Let them know where you're going, who you're with, and when you'll be back. This way, if you're not back on time, they'll know something's up and where to start looking for you.

So, that's all about staying connected and safe in the great outdoors. Remember, being able to communicate can turn you into a real-life wilderness hero!

BASIC WILDERNESS COMMUNICATION TOOLS

In the wilderness, staying connected is key. This means finding ways to communicate when there's no cell service. Let's explore some basic tools that can be lifesavers.

Whistles

A whistle is small but mighty. It's louder than your voice and can be heard from far away. If you're lost or in trouble, use the whistle to call for help. Here's how: blow three short blasts. This is a universal signal for help. Wait a bit, and then do it again. Keep doing this. It's like sending a loud message saying, "I'm here, and I need help!"

Mirrors

Mirrors are not just for checking your reflection. They can be a powerful tool to signal for help. Here's a cool trick: On a sunny day, hold the mirror so it catches the sun's rays. Then aim the shiny light at where you think people might be. Move it back and forth. This creates flashes that can be seen from miles away. It's like using the sun to send a bright, flashy text message.

Flags and Markers

You can make flags with anything bright and colorful. An orange jacket, a piece of cloth, or even a large leaf painted with bright colors works. Raise the flag high or place your markers in an open area. This way, rescuers can see them from a distance or even from the air. Think of it as putting up a big, colorful sign that says, "I'm over here!"

Natural Signs

You can also use what nature gives you. Arrange rocks or sticks on the ground to spell out an SOS or a big arrow pointing to where you are. You can even use your footprints to make a trail. It's like leaving breadcrumbs for someone to follow.

Keeping in Touch Before You Leave

Before you head out on your adventure, always tell someone where you're going, who you're with, and when you plan to return. This is super important. It's like leaving a treasure map so people know where to find you if you're late coming home.

Practicing with Your Tools

It's fun and important to practice using these tools. Try them out in a safe place, like your backyard or a park with an adult. Learn how to whistle loudly, flash a mirror, or make a flag. It's like training to be a wilderness detective.

Important Points to Remember

1. Always have these tools with you. You never know when you might need them.

2. Practice makes perfect. Get good at using them before you need them for real.

3. Stay calm. If you ever need to use them, staying calm will help you think clearly.

4. And remember, these tools are for real emergencies. Use them wisely and responsibly.

By learning these simple communication tools, you become smarter, safer, and more prepared for your outdoor adventures. It's empowering to know that with just a few basic items, you can send powerful messages across the wilderness. Stay safe, have fun, and explore the wonders of nature with confidence!

HOW TO SIGNAL SOS IN DIFFERENT FORMS

When exploring the great outdoors, knowing how to signal for help can be a game-changer. SOS is the universal distress signal, and it's easy to learn. It means "Save Our Souls" and it's a way to say "I need help" without using words. Let's dive into the different ways to signal SOS.

Visual Signals

One of the simplest ways to signal SOS is with visual cues. You can use anything that's visible. Here's how:

- Lights: If you have a flashlight or any light source, turn it on and off to create bursts of light. Follow the pattern: three short, three long, three short flashes. This pattern is internationally recognized as a call for help.

- Flags: If you have any piece of fabric, you can wave it in the SOS pattern. Just wave it quickly three times, slower three times, and quickly three times again.

- Nature's Canvas: If you're in a place with sand, snow, or even a clearing in the woods, you can draw the SOS signal. Make three short lines, three longer lines, and three short lines again. Make sure the lines are big and clear so they can be seen from above.

- Hand Signals: Do this hand gesture sequence, hand open, hand open with thumb in, and hand close over thumb.

SOS HAND SIGNALS

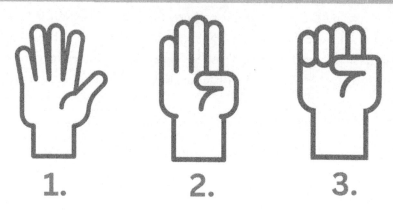

1.   **2.**   **3.**

Sound Signals

Sounds can travel far, especially in quiet places. Here's what you can do:

- Whistles: Just like with visual signals, blow your whistle three times quickly, pause, blow three long times, pause, and then three quick times again. Repeat this pattern.

- Voice: If you don't have a whistle, use your voice. Shout or sing in the same pattern as the whistle. It might not travel as far, but it's worth a try.

Modern Technology

In today's world, we have some cool gadgets that can help:

- Phones: Even if there's no signal to make calls, sometimes you can still send a text message with your location and an SOS message.

- Emergency Beacons: These are special devices that send an SOS signal to rescue teams. They work even where phones don't.

Preparation Is Key

Before heading out on your adventure, it's important to be prepared:

1. Learn the SOS Signal: Practice making the SOS signal in different ways. You can practice with lights, drawing it out, or even just tapping the pattern on a table.

2. Carry the Right Tools: Always have a whistle, a small mirror, or a flashlight with you. They are light and can be life-savers.

3. Tell Someone Your Plan: Make sure to tell someone where you're going, who you're with, and when you plan to return. It's important so that if you don't return on time, they know where to start looking.

By understanding how to signal SOS in different forms, you equip yourself with a crucial skill for outdoor adventures. It's empowering to know these simple techniques can make a big difference in staying safe. Remember, the wilderness is a wonderful place to explore, and being prepared makes it even better!

BASIC MORSE CODE

Morse code is a cool way to send messages using dots and dashes. It's like turning a flashlight or a sound into secret messages. People used it a long time ago to communicate over long distances, and it's still useful, especially in the wilderness.

Understanding Morse Code

Morse code turns each letter of the alphabet into a series of dots (short signals) and dashes (long signals). For example, the letter 'A' is a dot and a dash.

Spacing

- Between each dot and dash within a letter: Pause for a very short time, just long enough to start the next signal.

- Between letters: Leave a pause about as long as three dots.

- Between words: Make a longer pause, about as long as seven dots.

It's fun to learn and can be a great way to send a message if you're out of other options.

Letters of the alphabet in Mosecode:

A   dot-dash (· —)

B   dash-dot-dot-dot (— · · ·)

C   dash-dot-dash-dot (— · — ·)

D   dash-dot-dot (— · ·)

E   dot (·)

F   dot-dot-dash-dot (· · — ·)

G   dash-dash-dot (— — ·)

H   dot-dot-dot-dot (· · · ·)

I   dot-dot (· ·)

J   dot-dash-dash-dash (· — — —)

K   dash-dot-dash (— · —)

L   dot-dash-dot-dot (· — · ·)

M   dash-dash (— —)

N   dash-dot (— ·)

O   dash-dash-dash (— — —)

P   dot-dash-dash-dot (· — — ·)

Q   dash-dash-dot-dash (— — · —)

R   dot-dash-dot (· — ·)

S   dot-dot-dot (· · ·)

T   dash (—)

U   dot-dot-dash (· · —)

V   dot-dot-dot-dash (· · · —)

W   dot-dash-dash (· — —)

X   dash-dot-dot-dash (— · · —)

Y   dash-dot-dash-dash (— · — —)

Z   dash-dash-dot-dot (— — · ·)

You can create these signals in different ways, like flashing a light or tapping on a surface. It's like learning a new language, but with lights and sounds!

Making Words

Once you know some letters, try making words. Start with short words like 'SOS', which is dot-dot-dot, dash-dash-dash, dot-dot-dot. It's a universal distress signal. Remember to leave a

Practicing Morse Code

Practicing is key. You can use a flashlight to practice the dots and dashes in the dark. Or tap them out on a table. You can even turn it into a game with your friends or family.

Using Morse Code in the Wild

If you're in a situation where you need help and can't talk or yell, Morse code can be your voice. You can flash it with a light or make the sounds with a whistle. Remember, stay calm and go slow. It's important to make sure each dot and dash is clear.

Safety Tips

- Always carry a small flashlight or a whistle. These are your Morse code tools.

- Make sure to practice Morse code in a safe place before you need to use it.

Telling Someone About Your Adventure

Before you head out, tell someone your plans. Say where you're going, who you're with, and when you'll be back. This way, if you're late, they'll know something's up and where to find you.

Morse code is a unique and handy skill to have. It's not just about sending messages; it's about staying safe and being prepared for anything. Learning Morse code is like unlocking a secret skill that could one day be a big help. Happy coding!

USING TECHNOLOGY WISELY

In today's world, technology is everywhere, and it can be a big help when we're exploring the great outdoors. Devices like satellite phones, radios, and GPS units are not just cool gadgets; they're tools that can keep us safe and connected, even in the wildest places.

Satellite Phones

A satellite phone is a special kind of phone. It doesn't need cell towers to work. Instead, it talks to satellites in space. This means you can make calls from almost anywhere in the world, even in remote areas where regular phones don't work. If you get lost or need help, a satellite phone can be your lifeline.

Radios

Radios are another great tool. They let you talk to other people who have radios, and you don't need any cell service. Some radios even let you listen to weather reports. This can be super helpful to know if a storm is coming or if it's safe to continue your adventure.

GPS Devices

GPS stands for Global Positioning System. GPS devices use satellites to tell you exactly where you are on the planet. They can help you find your way if you get lost and can show you the path you've traveled. Some GPS devices also let you send messages or an SOS signal.

Using Tech Wisely

While these gadgets are helpful, it's important to use them wisely. Here are some tips:

1. **Learn Before You Go:** Understand how your device works before you go on your adventure. Practice using it at home.

2. **Keep Them Safe:** These devices are electronic, so keep them dry and safe. A waterproof bag or case is a good idea.

3. **Battery Life:** Always check the battery before you leave. Bring extra batteries or a way to charge your device.

4. **Have a Backup Plan:** Technology can fail. Batteries die, and gadgets can break. Always have a backup plan, like a map and a compass, and know how to use them.

Telling Someone About Your Adventure

Before you head out, always tell someone your plan. Let them know where you're going, who you're with, and when you plan to return. This way, if you don't come back on time, they'll know where to start looking for you.

Staying Safe and Connected

Satellite phones, radios, and GPS devices can make your adventures safer and more fun. They let you explore with confidence, knowing you can reach out for help or find your way back if you need to. Just remember, while technology is awesome, being prepared and knowing the basics of wilderness survival is still super important. Happy exploring!

EMERGENCY PHONE NUMBERS

When you're out exploring the world, it's important to know how to call for help if you need it. Different places around the world have different phone numbers for emergencies. These numbers are like magic keys that connect you to people who can help when you're in trouble.

Why Emergency Numbers Matter

Emergency numbers are important because they connect you to services like the police, fire department, or medical help. These services are always ready to help people who are hurt, lost, or in danger. Knowing these numbers is like having a safety net.

Emergency Numbers Around the World

- In the United States and Canada, the emergency number is 911.

- In the United Kingdom, it's 999 or 112.

- In Australia, you dial 000 for emergencies.

- In New Zealand, the number is 111.

- For European Union countries, 112 is the number you need.

- In Japan, the number is 110 for police and 119 for ambulance and fire.

- In India, you dial 100 for police, 101 for fire, and 102 for ambulance.

- In South Africa, it's 10111 for police and 10177 for ambulance.

These are just a few examples. It's a good idea to find out the emergency number for any country you visit.

Making the Call

If you ever need to call an emergency number, here's what to do:

1. Stay calm. Take a deep breath to help you think clearly.

2. Dial the emergency number.

3. Clearly explain what the problem is and where you are. Give as much detail as you can.

4. Listen to the instructions given to you on the phone.

5. Stay on the line until you're told it's okay to hang up.

Being Prepared

Before going on an adventure, especially to a new country, find out the emergency number for that place. Write it down or save it in a phone. It's also smart to tell someone about your travel plans. Let them know where you're going, who you're with, and when you plan to return.

Understanding the Role of Emergency Services

Emergency services are there to help in serious situations. It's important to only call these numbers for real emergencies. If you're lost, hurt, or see someone else who needs help, that's the time to call.

Emergency numbers are a crucial part of staying safe while exploring. By knowing how to use them, you add another layer of safety to your adventures. Remember, adventures are about having fun and discovering new things, but being safe and prepared is what makes them truly enjoyable.

CHAPTER 9

MENTAL TOUGHNESS

Exploring the great outdoors isn't just about physical strength; it's also about the power of the mind. Mental toughness is like a superpower that helps you handle challenges, big and small, that you might face in the wild. This chapter dives into the art of staying strong, calm, and positive, even when things get tough.

First up is **Stress Management in the Wild**. The wilderness can be unpredictable, and sometimes things don't go as planned. It's normal to feel stressed, but the secret lies in handling it effectively. Techniques like deep breathing, positive thinking, and taking one step at a time can turn stress into a steppingstone rather than a stumbling block.

Next, we'll explore **Goal Setting and Personal Challenges**. Setting goals is like drawing a map for your adventure. It's about knowing where you want to go and planning the steps to get there. Whether it's hiking a new trail, learning a new survival skill, or camping out for the first time, setting achievable goals makes the journey rewarding.

Finally, we'll discuss **Handling Isolation**. Sometimes, in the wilderness, you might feel alone or cut off, especially in remote areas. But remember, isolation is also an opportunity to get to know yourself better. We'll talk about strategies like keeping a journal, observing nature, and using your imagination to turn moments of loneliness into moments of self-discovery and peace.

Mental toughness is about resilience, creativity, and inner strength. It's about facing the wild with a spirit of adventure and a heart full of courage. So, let's get ready to strengthen our minds, just like we do our muscles, for the incredible journey ahead!

STRESS MANAGEMENT IN THE WILD

Being in the wilderness is an adventure full of excitement and surprises. However, sometimes, it can also bring challenges and stress. But worry not! Handling stress in the wild is a skill that anyone can learn. It's about staying calm, thinking clearly, and having fun along the way.

Understanding Stress

Stress is like carrying a heavy backpack. It can weigh you down and make your adventure less fun. It might come from getting lost, facing bad weather, or just worrying about what could go wrong. The first step in managing stress is recognizing it. It's okay to feel stressed; it happens to everyone, even the most experienced adventurers.

Breathing: Your Secret Weapon

When stress kicks in, your breath can be your best tool. Deep breathing helps calm your mind. Try this: breathe in slowly while counting to four, hold your breath for four seconds, then breathe out for four seconds. It's like hitting the reset button on your body's stress response.

Positive Thinking

Your thoughts have power. Instead of thinking about what could go wrong, focus on what can go right. Replace worries with hopeful thoughts. For instance, if you're worried about getting lost, think about how you've learned to read a map and use a compass.

One Step at a Time

Breaking big challenges into smaller steps makes them easier to handle. If you have a long hike ahead, don't think about the entire distance. Focus on getting to the next landmark, then the next. It's like completing a puzzle, one piece at a time.

Nature's Help

The wilderness itself is a great stress reliever. Take time to look around. Notice the trees, the sky, the birds. Nature's beauty can be a great distraction from your worries.

Talking It Out

If you're with others, talk about what's stressing you. Often, just saying it out loud can make it seem less scary. Plus, others might have good ideas or comforting words.

Be Prepared

Preparation is key to reducing stress. This means having the right gear, learning survival skills, and knowing your route. When you feel prepared, you'll feel more confident and less stressed.

Journaling

Keeping a journal can be a great way to manage stress. Write down your thoughts and feelings. It's a way to let them out and make sense of them.

Rest and Relax

Make sure to take breaks. Resting helps your body and mind recover. Enjoy a snack, hydrate, and relax for a bit before moving on.

Embrace the Experience

Remember, being in the wild is about adventure and learning. Every challenge is a chance to grow stronger and more skilled. Embrace these experiences, even the stressful ones. They are part of your journey.

Managing stress in the wild is all about staying calm, being positive, and taking things one step at a time. Remember, every adventurer faces stress, but it's how you handle it that makes all the difference. With these techniques, you're well on your way to becoming a confident and happy explorer, ready for whatever adventures lie ahead.

GOAL SETTING AND PERSONAL CHALLENGES

Setting goals and embracing personal challenges is like planning an exciting journey. It involves deciding where you want to go and how you're going to get there. In the wild, this isn't just about reaching a physical destination; it's about growing, learning new things, and becoming stronger, both inside and out.

The Power of Goals

Goals are like markers on a trail; they guide you and keep you on track. They can be big or small – from learning to light a fire without matches to completing a challenging hike. Achievable goals give you something to aim for and a sense of accomplishment when you reach them.

Start Small

Begin with small, easy goals. This could be identifying five different kinds of plants on your next hike or learning to tie a basic knot. Small victories build confidence and prepare you for bigger challenges.

Make It Personal

Your goals should be yours – something that excites and motivates you. Maybe you want to learn to navigate using a map and compass, or perhaps you're interested in identifying bird calls. Choose something that feels meaningful and fun to you.

Write It Down

Writing down your goals makes them real. Keep a journal of your goals and the steps you're taking to achieve them. It's a great way to track your progress and see how far you've come.

Challenging Yourself

Personal challenges are about stepping out of your comfort zone. It could be trying a new outdoor activity or going on a longer hike than usual. These challenges help you discover more about yourself and what you're capable of.

Celebrate Your Achievements

When you reach a goal, take a moment to celebrate. It could be as simple as sharing your achievement with a friend or family member. Celebrating makes the journey more enjoyable and rewarding.

Learning from Setbacks

Not every attempt will be a success, and that's okay. Setbacks are part of the journey. They teach resilience and problem-solving. The key is to learn from them and keep moving forward.

Setting New Goals

Once you achieve a goal, set a new one. It keeps the adventure going. Each goal is a step towards becoming more skilled, knowledgeable, and confident in the wild.

Sharing Your Goals

Share your goals with someone you trust, like a family member or a friend. They can offer support, advice, and encouragement. Plus, sharing your goals can inspire others to set their own.

Goal setting and embracing personal challenges in the wild are about more than just reaching a destination. They're about the journey of growing stronger, more confident, and more skilled. Every goal achieved and every challenge faced is a step forward in your adventure, not just in the wilderness, but in life too. So dream big, start small, and keep moving forward. The adventure is yours to create!

HANDLING ISOLATION

Finding oneself in the quiet embrace of nature, away from the bustling crowd, can be a rewarding experience. However, it can also bring feelings of loneliness or isolation, especially in remote areas. Developing strategies to manage these feelings is an essential part of wilderness adventures.

Embracing Solitude

Solitude, the state of being alone, doesn't have to be lonely. It can be a time for reflection, growth, and enjoying your own company. In the wilderness, embrace the quiet. Listen to the wind, watch the clouds, and observe the wildlife. This connection with nature can turn solitude into a peaceful, fulfilling experience.

Staying Connected

Even in remote areas, staying connected with loved ones can be comforting. If you have access to a phone or a radio, a quick call or message can bridge the distance. If not, thinking about good times shared with family and friends, or planning what to tell them about your adventure, can bring a sense of closeness.

Keeping Busy

An active mind doesn't have time to feel lonely. Plan activities to fill your time. It could be exploring, journaling, photography, bird watching, or learning new skills like knot tying or star navigation. These activities provide a sense of purpose and accomplishment.

Creativity and Imagination

Use your imagination to transform the experience. Create stories, draw, or write poetry inspired by your surroundings. Imaginative activities are not only fun but also a great way to express creativity and feelings.

Routine and Structure

Creating a routine helps manage feelings of isolation. Plan your days with structured activities, like setting up camp, cooking meals, or hiking to specific points. This structure provides a sense of normalcy and control.

Mindfulness and Meditation

Practicing mindfulness and meditation can be powerful in handling isolation. Focus on your breathing, be present in the moment, and acknowledge your thoughts and feelings without judgment. This practice helps in finding inner peace and contentment.

Exercise and Physical Activity

Physical activity is a great mood booster. Simple exercises, yoga, or a brisk walk can release endorphins, the body's natural feel-good chemicals. Exercise also helps in maintaining physical health, which is closely linked to mental well-being.

Reflecting on Personal Growth

Use this time to reflect on personal growth. Think about your strengths, achievements, and the new skills you're learning. Recognizing personal development brings a sense of pride and accomplishment.

Connecting with Nature

Sometimes, the best way to combat loneliness is to connect deeply with nature. Observe the patterns of the trees, the stars, or the behavior of animals. Feeling a part of the larger natural world can reduce feelings of isolation.

Handling isolation in the wild is about finding balance. It's about embracing solitude, staying connected in your own way, keeping busy, and finding peace within yourself. It's a journey that not only teaches resilience but also deepens your connection with the natural world. Remember, every moment alone is an opportunity to discover something new about yourself and the environment around you.

CONCLUSION

In this book, we've embarked on a journey to empower young explorers with essential survival skills, nurturing their connection with the great outdoors. At its heart, this guide is more than just a manual; it's a gateway to fostering independence, critical thinking, and a deep respect for nature among children aged 8-12. Through engaging, child-friendly lessons, we've aimed to demystify the wilderness, transforming it from a place of uncertainty to a playground of learning and adventure. This book stands as a testament to the belief that every child, equipped with the right knowledge and attitude, can become a confident and responsible outdoor enthusiast.

The key takeaways from this book are vital life lessons that extend beyond the wilderness. Firstly, safety is paramount. Children learn to prioritize safety in all aspects of life, understanding that preparation and awareness are key to avoiding and managing risks. Secondly, responsibility towards nature and oneself is emphasized. We teach children to respect the environment, leaving no trace behind and understanding the impact of their actions. Thirdly, the skills imparted instill confidence. From building a shelter to navigating by the stars, these skills empower children to feel capable and self-reliant. Additionally, problem-solving and adaptability are highlighted, as kids learn to think on their feet, adapting to various situations creatively and effectively. Finally, these survival skills, while practical in the wilderness, are also metaphorical tools for everyday life, teaching resilience, perseverance, and the value of learning through experience. This book equips young minds not just for outdoor adventures, but for life's unpredictable journey.

As we conclude, let's reflect on the story of Emma, a 10-year-old reader. On a family camping trip, Emma faced an unexpected challenge when her younger brother wandered off. Drawing upon the navigation skills she learned from our book, Emma remained calm, used landmarks to orient herself, and successfully led her brother back to their campsite. This real-life application of her newfound knowledge not only ensured their safety but also filled Emma with a sense of accomplishment and joy. Her story exemplifies the practical benefits of our lessons and the transformative power of outdoor exploration, igniting a lifelong passion for adventure and learning in the natural world.

Now, dear young adventurers, it's your turn to step into the great outdoors. Remember, "Survival Skills for Kids" is your companion in this exciting journey. Start with small adventures, perhaps a hike in a local park or a night of camping in your backyard. Each page you've turned in this book has equipped you with knowledge and skills; now apply them in real life. Build your confidence step by step, adventure by adventure. The wilderness is a vast classroom, and you are its eager student. So, lace up your boots, pack your bag, and embark on your journey with curiosity and courage. The world awaits your explorations!

As you embark on your outdoor adventures, we'd love to hear about your experiences with Survival Skills for Kids. Your feedback is invaluable, not just to us, but to other young explorers and their families. Please take a moment to share your thoughts and reviews. Your journey could inspire many more!

Printed in Great Britain
by Amazon

44015488R00076